DICTATORSHIPS

OMAR AL-BASHIR'S

SUDAN

DIANA CHILDRESS

TWENTY-FIRST CENTURY BOOKS | **MINNEAPOLIS**

To Wayne Furman and David Smith, gatekeepers to the sanctum sanctorum for writers in New York City, the Frederick Lewis Allen Memorial Room of the New York Public Library, with many thanks for your support and encouragement

Consultant: Carolyn Fluehr-Lobban, Ph.D., professor of Anthropology, Rhode Island College, and editor, *Bulletin of the Sudan Studies Association*.

Twenty-First Century Books
A division of Lerner Publishing Group, Inc.
241 First Avenue North
Minneapolis, MN 55401 U.S.A.

Website address: www.lernerbooks.com

Library of Congress Cataloging-in-Publication Data

Childress, Diana.
    Omar al-Bashir's Sudan / by Diana Childress.
        p.   cm. — (Dictatorships)
    Includes bibliographical references and index.
    ISBN 978-0-8225-9096-5 (lib. bdg. : alk. paper)
        1. Bashir, 'Umar Hasan Ahmad, 1944- —Juvenile literature.
    2. Presidents—Sudan—Biography—Juvenile literature. 3. Dictators—
    Sudan—Biography—Juvenile literature. 4. Sudan—Politics and
    government—1985- —Juvenile literature. 5. Sudan—Social conditions—
    Juvenile literature. I. Title.
    DT157.673.C47 2010
    962.404'3092—dc22 [B]   2008053931

Manufactured in the United States of America
1 2 3 4 5 6 – DP – 15 14 13 12 11 10

CONTENTS

A LIGHTNING

DURING THE SUMMER OF 1989, the African country of Sudan was in turmoil. In the south, rebel forces were fighting against government troops in a devastating civil war.

The south wanted three things. One was the right to choose its own regional and local government. This right, granted by Sudan's constitution, had been abolished by a military dictator. The second demand was to end Sharia, a legal system based on the religious writings of Islam. In 1983 the same dictator had imposed this Islamic law on all Sudanese, including southerners. Most southerners were not Muslims but Christians or followers of a traditional African religion. They did not want to be subjected to laws based on a religion they did not practice. The third demand was the fair distribution of economic development and the wealth from Sudan's natural resources. Foreign companies had discovered oil in the south, but northerners

COUP

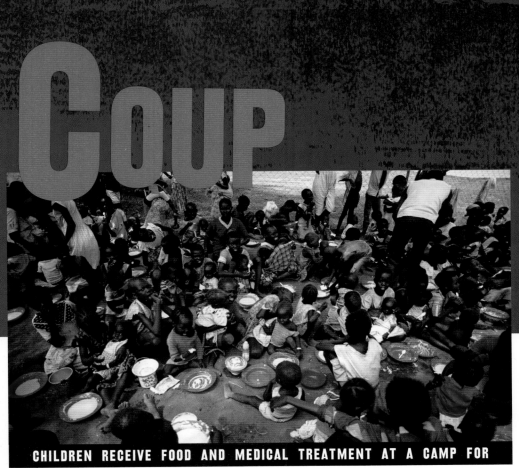

CHILDREN RECEIVE FOOD AND MEDICAL TREATMENT AT A CAMP FOR displaced people in southern Sudan in 1989. Years of war and famine drove people in the southern part of the country from their homes.

had taken charge of developing the industry. Southerners feared that only northerners would benefit from the profits.

The war was in its sixth year. The south was gaining ground, under the leadership of Colonel John Garang, a former officer of the Sudanese army. But drought had brought widespread famine to the area. According to an international relief agency, 250,000 southern Sudanese died from war, disease, and hunger in 1988. Two to three million more fled from their homes, villages, and farms. They, too, were in danger of starvation.

At the head of the government of Sudan was Prime Minister Sadiq al-Mahdi, the leader of the Umma Party. When the country democratically elected him to office in 1986, he had promised peace. But he did not keep his campaign promises. Instead, in early 1987, he escalated the war by recruiting new militias. Many poor, unemployed, and discontented young men herded cattle in the region of the north-south border. The drought had made it hard for these nomads to find pasture for their herds, and they resented the southern farmers, who were also poor but who at least had land. Taking advantage of the simmering tensions between herders and farmers, Prime Minister Sadiq al-Mahdi armed the herdsmen with automatic weapons. He ordered them to attack the farmers, especially those who belonged to the Dinka ethnic group (the same group as the rebel leaders), on the pretext that they were supporting the rebel forces. Since the government lacked the money to pay the new militias, he gave them the right to pay themselves by looting. The result was a disaster for millions of southern civilians, especially the Dinka but other ethnic groups as well.

As the south bled and burned, Sadiq al-Mahdi made long-winded speeches on television about Sudan's problems. The Sudanese economy crashed, hit hard by military spending, drought, and corruption. Even in northern Sudan, food became scarce, and prices for flour, sugar, bread, and other everyday necessities skyrocketed. Newspaper editorials accused the government of inaction, dishonesty, and greed. Citizens poured out into city streets yelling for Sadiq to "shut up and do something!"

Then, overnight, everything changed. At two in the morning on June 30, 1989, under cover of darkness, Sudanese army tanks and armored personnel carriers rolled out across the streets of the capital, Khartoum, and its neighboring cities of Omdurman and Khartoum North. Troops took over government buildings, the presidential palace, the airport, and the bridges crossing the Nile River. Military police arrested hundreds of politicians, government workers, and trade union leaders. All across Sudan, army units occupied government buildings.

On July 1, Sudanese awoke to martial music on state-owned Radio Omdurman and news of a dusk-to-dawn curfew. The capital was calm. "You see armed guards nearly everywhere," one man reported. "There are roadblocks on many streets, but the soldiers are quite easygoing. Most pedestrians are being allowed to proceed freely."

That afternoon an unfamiliar man's voice announced the coup over the radio. Introducing himself as Brigadier General Omar Hassan Ahmed al-Bashir, he said that a fifteen-member Revolutionary Command Council for National Salvation now ruled Sudan. As the new "head of state, minister of defense and commander of the armed forces," Bashir declared the constitution suspended and ordered all political parties immediately dissolved.

No one knew what to expect of this surprising new leader. Bashir did not hold high command in the army. The colleagues he named as members of his council were all midlevel army officers like himself. Forty-five-year-old Bashir was the oldest of the group. He had no known political ties. In fact, all the general public knew about him was that he had carried out a well-planned, bloodless coup and seemed to be in full control of the army and the government of Sudan. Not knowing whether to be relieved that Sadiq's waffling was over or to fear for the future, the Sudanese waited to see what would happen next.

CHAPTER 1

A DIVERSE LAND

SUDAN IS THE LARGEST NATION IN AFRICA. With an area of close to 1 million square miles (2.5 million square kilometers), it is about the size of the United States east of the Mississippi. Sudan embraces a broad range of African environments, from bone-dry desert in the north to humid rain forest in the south. In between stretch broad bands of semiarid Sahel and grassy savanna. Because the entire country lies in the tropical zone near the equator, temperatures vary little. Most of the year is hot. Summer temperatures in Khartoum can soar to 115°F (46°C). Much of the country is flat, but a few mountainous regions rise above the plains: the Red Sea Hills to the northeast, the Marra range to the west, the Imatong Mountains to the south, and the Nuba Mountains in south central Sudan.

The Nile River is the outstanding geographical feature of Sudan. Flowing from south to north, it drains the water of many rivers.

AND PEOPLE

THE NILE RIVER IS IMPORTANT to the people of Sudan. It makes the desert habitable, and dams along the river provide electricity.

Its principal branches are the White Nile and the Blue Nile. The White Nile is named for the whitish sediment of its riverbed and the Blue Nile for its dark blue black color at full flood.

The longest branch, the White Nile, enters Sudan from the highlands of Uganda. It crashes down in great leaps and bounds through Sudan's southernmost states. On reaching the flat plains of the savanna, it splits up into a maze of shifting watercourses and tall reeds. The river becomes a vast swamp called the Sudd. Tributary rivers, the Bahr al-Arab from the west and the Sobat from the east, help push it back on its northward course through the increasingly drier landscapes of the Sahel.

The rapid waters of the Blue Nile descend from Ethiopia. After the river crosses into Sudan, two dams harness its flow to create electrical power and provide irrigation for central Sudan. At Khartoum the Blue Nile and the White Nile join to form the Nile River.

Leaving Khartoum, the Nile snakes through the desert in a large lazy S, stretching the 450-mile (725 km) distance to the Egyptian border into a 1,000-mile (1,600 km) journey. A final tributary, the Atbara, joins the river along the way. Rocks and rapids limit boat traffic along this part of the river, but the flowing water makes the desert habitable. Below what is called the third cataract (a waterfall or steep rapids), the river flows into Lake Nubia, an enormous reservoir. The lake was created by Egypt's Aswan High Dam, which was completed in 1971. A large dam recently opened at Merowe on the fourth cataract.

WHO ARE THE SUDANESE?

Hundreds of ethnic groups, many subdivided into clans, live in Sudan. Some came to Sudan from other parts of Africa or across the Red Sea from the Arabian Peninsula. A long history of migration and intermarriage has made the Sudanese a mix of southwest Asian, North African, and African peoples from south of the Sahara. Their skin color ranges from light brown to black, and other physical features also vary. Some Sudanese resemble Egyptians or Arabs, while others

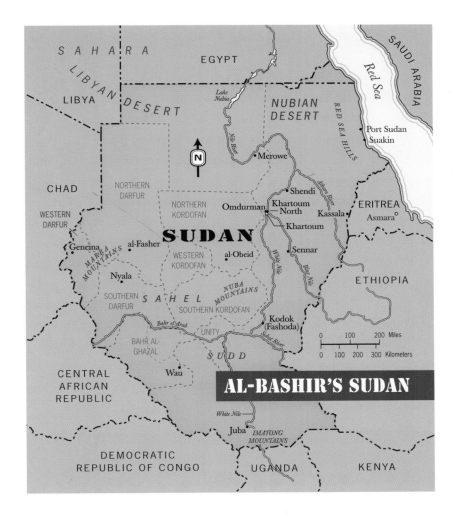

AL-BASHIR'S SUDAN

share many traits with people from western and central Africa.

About 70 percent of Sudanese belong to the Sunni, or main branch of Islam, and Islam is the dominant religion in the northern two-thirds of the country. About 5 percent of Sudanese are Christians. Most live in southern Sudan or in Khartoum. Other Sudanese practice traditional religions, sometimes mixed with Christian beliefs, and live primarily in southern Sudan.

The official languages of Sudan are Arabic and English. The majority of Sudanese also speak one or more ethnic languages or dialects. According to the Sudan Institute of Languages, 132 different languages are spoken in Sudan. Some of these languages have been adopted by state and local governments as additional official languages.

To Americans who expect people of different races to look different, the racial and ethnic distinctions the Sudanese make can be confusing. Some Sudanese ethnic distinctions are regional. The Beja, Fur, Rizeigat, and Dinka groups have long been associated with different regions of the country. Other distinctions are occupational. A number of different groups belong to the Baqqara, who are seminomadic cattle herders, or the Abbala, who are camel herders. Although loyal to different leaders, members of these herding groups share economic concerns—such as access to pastures and water for their livestock—and they band together to address them.

ISLAM

Islam is a monotheistic (worshipping a single god) religion based on the teachings of the prophet Muhammad, an Arab religious and political leader who died in 632. Islam means "submission," and followers of Islam are known as Muslims, or "those who submit to God." In the late 600s, disagreements over the leadership of the Muslim community led to a division into two major denominations, the Sunni (about 85 percent of Muslims) and

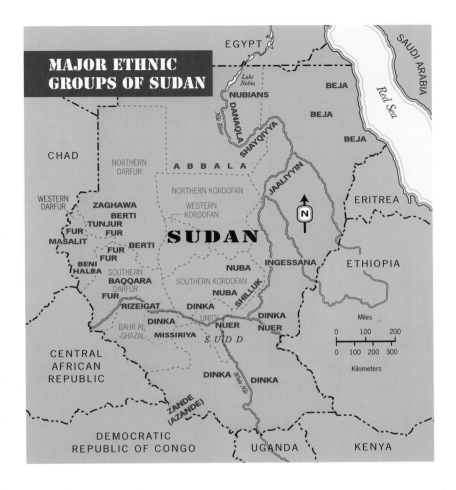

MAJOR ETHNIC
GROUPS OF SUDAN

The most confusing distinction to non-Sudanese is between Arab and African. This opposition is basically cultural. "Arab" Sudanese self-identify with Arab culture. They may have or claim to have ancestors from the Arabian Peninsula. They speak Arabic as their primary language, wear Arabic-style clothing, and follow Islam. To foreigners, they may look no different from "African" Sudanese. The "African" Sudanese consider themselves African. They may or may not be Muslim, and Arabic may or may not be their mother tongue.

EARLY CIVILIZATIONS

Sudan has a long and complex history that stretches back thousands of years. Early humans hunted and gathered wild foods along the Nile about 150,000 years ago. During periods when the climate was wetter, between 12,000 and 8,000 years ago, people settled all across northern Sudan. As the climate dried, they moved closer to the rivers. Four thousand years ago, a major civilization began to develop along the Nile in this area. The Egyptians to the north called it the Kingdom of Kush, but the people living there called themselves Nubians.

The Nubian people living along the palm-lined banks of the Nile became prosperous trading in gold, ivory, and slaves. Their rulers built great temples and pyramids. By the eighth century B.C., the kingdom was powerful enough for Nubian armies to march north and triumph over Egypt. For almost a hundred years, Nubian pharaohs ruled an empire that reached from the Mediterranean Sea to modern Khartoum. Their fame spread across the ancient world. The Egyptians later drove the Nubians back to Sudan, where their culture flourished until the fourth century A.D.

THIS NUBIAN MONUMENT IN Egypt shows one of the Nubian rulers of the empire. The Nubian people lived along the Nile.

After the Nubian civilization declined, a number of small king-doms developed along northern Sudan's Nile Valley. Some of their kings converted to Christianity.

THE ARRIVAL OF ISLAM

In the eighth century, Islam began to arrive in Sudan. The religion, which arose in the seventh century on the Arabian Peninsula, came with Arab merchants, who traveled across the Red Sea from Arabia and overland from Egypt. Many of these traders settled in Sudan and married Sudanese women. Islam gradually spread across northeastern Sudan. By the fourteenth century, these Arab immigrants were numerous and powerful enough to overthrow the Christian kings. In time, much of the Nile Valley in northern Sudan became home to mixed-race Arabic-speaking Muslims.

While the Arabs settled the north, two indigenous kingdoms were expanding in central and western Sudan. The Funj people formed a loosely organized domain. At its greatest extent, it reached from the southern edge of the Nubian Desert (part of the Sahara that lies east of the Nile) up the Nile to modern Khartoum and farther south along both the Blue Nile toward the Ethiopian highlands and the White Nile toward the swamps of southern Sudan. Funj rulers converted to Islam but retained many traditional African rituals and beliefs as well, such as belief in the leader's divinity. About 1650 they established their capital at Sennar on the Blue Nile. There they built a walled city with a grand royal palace, five stories tall.

In western Sudan, Fur people living in the Marra mountain range gained control over a large area that came to be known as

Dar Fur (land of the Fur). Establishing their capital at al-Fasher, Fur rulers levied taxes on caravan goods traveling between western Africa and Egypt. They developed a strong central government that dominated the modern regions of Darfur and Kordofan.

Like the Funj, the Fur adopted Islam, and the rulers of both kingdoms took the Muslim title of sultan. Sons of Fur and Funj leaders traveled to Egypt for religious studies in Cairo. Islamic teachers came from Arabia and Egypt to Sudan and established brotherhoods of followers. Sudanese scholars learned to speak and write Arabic, but Arabic did not replace the Fur and Funj languages.

SLAVERY

Both sultanates (areas ruled by sultans), as well as the smaller Arab states in northern Sudan, depended heavily on slave labor and slave trading. Since the Quran—the holy book of Islam—forbids the enslavement of Muslims, Muslim slave traders looked to southern Sudan, where people practiced traditional African religions. People in southern Sudan lived in small villages, organized into clans. Chiefs and village elders ruled these groups. Since the area did not have large kingdoms or extreme class differences, slavery did not play a major role in their societies. They did enslave prisoners they captured in local wars, and chiefs were willing to exchange them for goods such as metal tools and weapons brought by traders from northern Sudan.

Such small trades, however, did not meet the demands of the sultans. To gain more slaves, rulers licensed slavers to raid villages in specific areas south of their kingdoms and capture people for the slave market. Some groups on the southern edges of the sultanates organized their own slave raids so that they could pay the slavers an annual tribute in slaves and thus avoid capture themselves.

The slave trade in Sudan was so lucrative, it attracted the attention of powerful neighbors to the north. During the sixteenth to the eighteenth centuries—when the Funj and Fur kingdoms were flourishing—the Ottoman Turks ruled a huge empire based in Istanbul, Turkey. At its peak, the Ottoman Empire embraced all North Africa, the eastern half of the Mediterranean Sea, parts of eastern Europe, and western Asia as far east of Istanbul as Iraq. Rulers and upper classes in this large empire depended on slaves for military troops, domestic servants, and agricultural labor.

THE TURKIYYA, 1820–1881

By the nineteenth century, the Ottoman Empire was in decline, but an ambitious Ottoman viceroy (a governor who rules an area as the representative of a king or emperor) ruled Egypt. This viceroy, Muhammad Ali, saw opportunities in Sudan. Eager to gain control of the slave trade and access to Sudanese gold mines, he invaded Sudan in 1820.

Confronted by the large, well-armed Turkish-Egyptian expedition, the sultan of Funj quickly surrendered. The Turkish-led troops also captured the region of Kordofan from the sultan of Darfur and, fifty years later, Darfur as well. Once in control of northern and central Sudan, the Turks advanced up the Nile through the swampy area known as the Sudd. Although they never conquered the Shilluk, Dinka, Nuer, and other groups of southern Sudan, they

> "You are aware that the end of all our effort and this expense is to procure Negroes. Please show zeal in carrying out our wishes in this capital matter."
>
> —Muhammad Ali, viceroy of Egypt, to Muhammad Bey Khusraw, the commander of his armies in Sudan, September 23, 1825

added to outsiders' knowledge of the area and claimed it as part of their colony.

In this way, Turkish rule (which the Sudanese called the Turkiyya) brought most of modern Sudan together under one government for the first time. For sixty-five years, Ottoman viceroys in Cairo ruled Sudan. Some of the early governor-generals they appointed brutalized the Sudanese, taxing them heavily, massacring populations that opposed Turkish rule, or forcing them into slavery. In 1839, however, the Ottoman sultan launched a number of measures known as the Tanzimat (reorganization) reforms to modernize the empire. Sudan benefited from these progressive laws.

A governor-general and four regional governors led the Turkiyya. Egyptian civil servants worked for them, and a few Sudanese held the lowest government posts.

The Turks established their capital at Khartoum—Arabic for "elephant's trunk"—named for a long, tapering stretch of land between the White Nile and Blue Nile, just south of the city. They successfully developed the Nile Valley. Agriculture flourished. Extensive plantations of fruit trees, sugarcane, indigo, and cotton flanked the river.

The viceroys of Egypt had been educated in Europe, where they witnessed the rapidly growing wealth brought by the Industrial Revolution. Eager to modernize their domains, they brought European engineers to Egypt and Sudan. In 1855 the first steamboat churned its way up the Nile from Cairo to Khartoum, giving Sudan swifter access to distant markets. In the 1870s, the first cotton gin sped up the separation of the cotton fibers from the seedpods and sticky seeds. Soon telegraph wires linked Khartoum to Cairo, the Red Sea port of Suakin, and al-Obeid in Kordofan. Leaders were planning railroad links as well.

To administer their expanding territory, the viceroys appointed many Europeans both to develop trade and to govern regions of Sudan. The Europeans who came to Sudan opposed the slave trade. Although the British had dominated the Atlantic slave trade in the eighteenth century, in 1807 abolitionists in Britain successfully brought about the end of legal slave trading in the British Empire. Several other European nations joined Britain in opposing slavery. Bowing to public opinion in Europe, in 1877 the viceroy agreed to end slavery in Sudan. Abolition, however, was impossible to enforce. Egyptian and Sudanese slave traders had private armies to protect their trading stations in southern Sudan, and demand for slaves was still high throughout the Ottoman Empire.

THE MAHDIST REVOLUTION

Although modernization and commerce enriched some Sudanese, resentment of Turkish-Egyptian rule smoldered in many parts of the colony. In 1881 the various opposition forces gained a charismatic leader, Muhammad Ahmad. He united the rebel groups and inspired a revolution against foreign domination.

Muhammad Ahmad was a religious leader from northern Sudan, famous for his holiness and strict opposition to materialism. He founded a religious center on Aba Island in the White Nile south of Khartoum. His disciples gathered there to hear his sermons denouncing Turkish immorality. In 1881 he sent letters to government officials declaring that he was the Expected Mahdi. In Islamic tradition, the Mahdi is a divine leader chosen by God at the end of time to overthrow evil and bring justice to humankind.

The Mahdi and his circle opposed Turkish rule, not because it was foreign or oppressive but because they believed it did not honor and enforce the Holy Law of Islam. The Turks were Muslims, but they had introduced Hanafi legal traditions to Sudan. The Hanafi is one of the most liberal schools of legal thought in Islam, known for its tolerance of differences within Muslim communities.

Other rebels who joined the Mahdi had less religious motives. Slave merchants became Mahdists because abolition threatened their livelihood. The Baqqara (the seminomadic cattle herders) backed the Mahdi because they resented the taxes Turkish officials imposed on them. Together they formed the fighting forces of the Mahdist revolution.

Over the next three years, the Mahdist army took Kordofan, Darfur, Bahr al-Ghazal (a region south of Darfur and Kordofan), Nubia in northern Sudan, and the Red Sea Hills to the northeast. By 1884 Mahdist forces were closing in on the central Nile Valley.

Meanwhile, British forces occupied Egypt in 1882 to help the viceroy put down a revolt there. The British owned a major interest in the Suez Canal, a strategic waterway completed in 1869 that links the Mediterranean to the Red Sea. The canal gave Europe easier access to markets and colonies in Asia. Although the British assumed military control of Egypt, they were reluctant to take over Sudan as well because of the Mahdist war. In 1884 the British sent General Charles Gordon, who had earlier served as a governor of Sudan, to evacuate the remaining Turkish and Egyptian forces garrisoned at Khartoum. Once there, however, Gordon decided he could defeat the Mahdi and sent for reinforcements. In January 1885, before British help arrived, the Mahdists attacked and defeated the defenders of Khartoum. Gordon was killed and the city destroyed.

MAHDIST SUDAN

The Mahdi died after a brief illness, five months after the fall of Khartoum. Khalifa Abdallahi, the military leader of the cattle nomads, succeeded the Mahdi as head of the government. The Mahdi's mission to spread "true Islam" was soon replaced by the need to keep control over the country. The khalifa became an efficient but harsh ruler, making all appointments and decisions and surrounding himself with armed bodyguards and a walled compound.

The principal threat to the khalifa's rule, however, was not regional rebellion but the European "Scramble for Africa." To the east, the Italians had taken Eritrea and were expanding into Sudan, capturing Kassala, on the Eritrean border, in 1894. The Belgians, installed in the Congo, were eyeing southern Sudan. The French were spreading from western Africa into Bahr al-Ghazal and envisioning a transcontinental French railroad from the Atlantic Ocean to the Red Sea. But the most serious challenge came from the north. The British, who still had an army in Egypt to protect the Suez Canal, now worried that the French would gain control of the Nile in Sudan. In 1896 the commander of the Anglo-Egyptian army, General Horatio Herbert Kitchener, began moving British and Egyptian troops across the Sudanese border. He worked his way up the Nile the following year, building a railroad as he went.

The Sudanese troops retreated southward but made a stand in

THE SCRAMBLE FOR AFRICA

Europeans had long traded along the coasts of Africa, occasionally establishing settlements and forts to protect trade. Portugal began colonizing Angola and Mozambique in the sixteenth century. The Dutch created the Cape Colony in South Africa in 1652 (which passed to British control in 1814), and the French moved into Algeria in 1830. Few other countries formed colonies in Africa before the 1880s.

Between the 1880s and 1914, however, European powers rapidly expanded existing settlements inland and claimed new regions. European nations wanted colonies as a source of cheap labor and valuable raw materials—gold and other metals, diamonds, food crops, and cotton. Colonies also provided markets for European-manufactured goods—textiles, clothing, railways, and all kinds of machines and machine parts. The competition among European countries to secure colonies in Africa was intense as they sliced up almost the entire African continent among themselves. France, Great Britain, Germany, Portugal, Belgium, Spain, and Italy all participated in this enormous land grab, which came to be

River in 1898. The British killed thousands of Sudanese with machine guns at one of the last battles between the British and Sudanese.

April 1898 at the Atbara River, about 150 miles (240 km) northeast of Khartoum. British machine guns mowed down the Sudanese troops by the thousands. Five months later, a second decisive battle on the Karari plain north of Omdurman sealed Kitchener's victory.

THE SECOND TURKIYYA

The British never officially made Sudan a colony. Instead they referred to their presence there as a corule called the Anglo-Egyptian Condominium. But although both flags flew over government buildings, Egypt's only role was to provide troops to enforce British policy. Much of British policy focused on law and order. A British governor-general led the government and ruled by decree. Laws officially abolished slave trading, but the trade never fully died out. Treaties with neighboring countries gradually established the modern boundaries of Sudan.

Many Sudanese referred to British rule as the second Turkiyya. Much as the Turks had done, the British brought development to central Sudan, building dams, irrigation projects, and railways. In 1902 they established Gordon Memorial College, a school in Khartoum to train Sudanese as civil servants for the condominium. Peripheral areas, such as the Nuba Mountains in Kordofan, Darfur, and southern Sudan, however, still suffered serious neglect. The British entrusted the government in these areas to leaders of local ethnic groups, a system the British called indirect rule. Instead of a British or educated Sudanese official from Khartoum, traditional sheikhs, nazirs, and umdas maintained law and order. British district officers assigned to these areas acted only as advisers and did little to modernize society.

In the south, where there were few Muslims, the British gave

"[Sudan is] the artificial product of military conquest, political bargains and whims of geographers . . . a country with no common nationality and a full measure of diversity."

—Harold Alfred MacMichael, British colonial administrator in Anglo-Egyptian Sudan from 1905 to 1933 grants to Christian missionaries from Europe to open schools. In these schools, southern children learned English, not Arabic, the language taught in northern Sudan. After 1922 any movement between north and south required special permits, further isolating southern Sudanese from their northern compatriots.

OPPOSING BRITISH RULE

The Sudanese chafed under British domination and soon began to demand a greater role in government. In 1924 a discontented young army officer formed a Sudanese nationalist movement called the White Flag League. The league organized demonstrations and armed resistance to British rule, but their efforts were quickly put down by British troops.

In 1938 more than a thousand graduates of Gordon Memorial College took a more diplomatic approach by forming the Graduates' General Congress. Although the British gave the organization no official role in the government, they allowed the congress to offer views on educational and social issues. Several political leaders emerged from this gathering of Sudan's educated elite. All wanted freedom from British rule, but they soon split into two factions. One favored uniting with Egypt against the British. The other sought a separate, independent Sudan.

World War II (1939–1945) interrupted Sudan's push for independence. In June 1940, Italy declared war on France and Britain, and Italian troops in Italy's colonies in present-day Eritrea and Libya moved into British-held Egypt and Sudan. On the eastern front, Sudanese troops (known as the Sudan Defense Force) fighting under

British command took Eritrea in 1941. The Sudan Defense Force also fought with the French against incursions into Sudan and Chad from Italian Libya. A more serious danger was the possibility of a German invasion from the north. Sudanese patrols worked with British intelligence agents to prevent German commandos from entering Sudan to contact Sudanese rebels and stir up anger against the British.

But while Britain battled Germany in both Europe and Africa, Sudan's politicians continued their efforts to gain a greater voice in governing Sudan. In 1942 the Graduates' Congress demanded that the government grant Sudan "the right of self-determination, directly after this war." The British refused to consider the idea, partly because they resented Sudan's political opposition at a time when British troops were fighting to defend the country.

INDEPENDENCE FOR SUDAN

After the war, in 1948, the British allowed the Sudanese to form a legislative assembly. Elections were held, and for the first time, southerners were included in a Sudanese congress. The assembly had no real power, as the British governor-general could veto its decisions. Nonetheless, it gave Sudanese political leaders a platform to campaign for independence. Political parties emerged, several of them linked to religious brotherhoods. The Mahdi's son, Abd al-Rahman al-Mahdi, led one of the largest parties, the Umma Party.

In 1952 a military coup in Egypt overthrew the monarchy that the British had established when it granted Egypt independence in 1922. The new military rulers—unlike the Egyptian king—favored self-government for Sudan. The Sudanese legislative assembly also chose self-government in a close vote. These political events led the British finally to agree to a transition to independence for Sudan. Elections were held for a constituent assembly to draft a constitution for the new government. In August 1955, this new parliament demanded that British and Egyptian forces leave Sudan. By November all the troops were gone. The last British governor-general left Sudan in December 1955.

On January 1, 1956, the Egyptian and British flags were lowered in Khartoum, and Sudan declared itself a sovereign democratic republic. A five-member Supreme Commission replaced the governor-general. The new Sudanese pound (the first Sudanese currency since Mahdist rule) replaced the British pound, and the first census established the population at 10.2 million. For the first time in Sudan's long history, the Sudanese people were free to govern themselves.

THE BRITISH AND EGYPTIAN flags are lowered from the palace at Khartoum in January 1956.

Many Sudanese must have watched proudly as the new Sudanese flag—three horizontal bars, blue over yellow over green—rose on Independence Day. The blue bar symbolized the Nile and its tributaries; the yellow, Sudan's deserts; and the green, its thriving agriculture. One likely observer that day was Omar Hassan Ahmed al-Bashir. It was his twelfth birthday.

CHAPTER 2

INDEPENDENT

OMAR HASSAN AHMED AL-BASHIR WAS BORN IN HOSH BANNAGA, a village along the Nile near Shendi about 100 miles (160 km) northeast of Khartoum. His birth, on January 1, 1944, came just two years after the Graduates' Congress presented the British governor of Sudan with a demand for self-rule.

Omar's father was a farmer. Like most Sudanese living in the area, the family belongs to the Jaaliyyin. This ethnic group descended from Arab immigrants who settled in the Nile Valley in the sixteenth and seventeenth centuries and married Nubian women. The Jaaliyyin trace their ancestry back to the early followers of the prophet Muhammad in Arabia.

Omar attended the local elementary school, where he learned to read and write Arabic, the local language. Part of his education was religious, but it also included secular subjects such as arithmetic.

SUDAN

THESE CHILDREN POSE FOR THE camera in Sudan in 1949. Sudanese children had more opportunities for education after World War II.

By the time Sudan won its independence, on Omar's twelfth birthday, Omar was commuting to Shendi to attend a private intermediate school. After World War II, Sudan increased the number of schools in the country to meet the needs of a soon-to-be independent nation. With British and Egyptians officials leaving the country, many government positions were opening up. Sudanese families were eager to educate their sons for possible employment in the new government. Job prospects were especially favorable for the Jaaliyyin because many educated elite who had worked for the British belonged to that group.

A DIVIDED COUNTRY

While Omar was growing up, the central problem facing the new country was the lack of national unity. The British had administered the north and south as though they were two separate colonies. This policy isolated the south from the north, increased the differences between northern and southern Sudanese, and prevented the development of nationwide patriotic feelings.

The first census ever, taken in 1956, showed that northerners outnumbered southerners by a ratio of almost 3 to 1. The north also had more cities, roads, railways, industry, and commercial agriculture. Northerners had better access to education—the only universities were in Khartoum—and played a greater role in government. Most Sudanese who worked as clerks, inspectors, tax collectors, and teachers for the British came from the Nile Valley. They were highly educated and knew the country well, as their jobs had sent them to all parts of Sudan. They were clearly the best equipped to take over running the country when it gained independence. Southerners, as well as northerners from communities far from the Nile rivers, lacked these advantages.

When a parliament was elected in 1953 to carry out the transition to independence, the Southern Party won only nine of the ninety-seven seats. Although more than one-quarter of the

> *"Well, as it appears, it means our fellow Northerners want to colonize us [southerners] for another one hundred years."*
>
> —Gregoria Denk Kir, southern Sudanese merchant, on hearing news that northern Sudanese had been appointed to 794 of 800 government posts, 1953

population lived in the south, less than one-tenth of the parliament specifically represented their interests. That lack of representation showed clearly the next year when a parliamentary committee was appointed to select Sudanese to replace British and Egyptian officials in eight hundred nonelective government posts. The committee assigned all but six of the positions to northerners.

An incident in the summer of 1955 revealed the deep mistrust southerners felt for northern Sudanese. As British and Egyptian troops pulled out of Sudan, a battalion of southern troops of the Sudan Defense Force was about to be transferred to the north. Rumors spread among the troops that they would be imprisoned or massacred there. Fearing the worst, the soldiers broke into the arms depot. They seized weapons and ammunition and began killing all northerners in the town where they were stationed. The mutiny quickly spread, causing riots in several southern garrisons. The army soon put the rebellion down, but the incident worsened relations between north and south.

A MULTIPARTY DEMOCRACY

When Sudanese rule began in January 1956, deep differences divided political leaders in the north as well. Two major parties represented Islamic sects with large followings. One, the Umma, looked to Europe and the United States for models. The other, the National Unionist Party (NUP), was more tied to Egypt, at that time ruled by General Gamal Nasser, a pro-Arab dictator. These two parties had led the transition parliament. But that year, the People's Democratic Party (PDP) split off from the NUP to form a new party. It later formed a coalition with the Umma.

The PDP-Umma alliance was not successful. Fundamental differences prevented the coalition from making progress in many areas, especially drafting a constitution for Sudan. Southern politicians, meanwhile, tried to gain support for a federal system of government that would give the south greater self-rule in local matters, such as health, education, and police. Freedom of religion was another important concern in the south. Northern politicians promised to consider these issues, but other problems took precedence.

When the first elections after independence were held in 1958, the Umma again won the most seats in parliament and continued its coalition with the PDP. The Southern Liberal Party (the new name of the Southern Party) gained forty seats, almost a quarter of the total. But bickering between members of the two coalition parties again stalled progress. By November it was clear that the two factions were too busy maneuvering for political power to govern the country. It was the first of several failures of parliamentary democracy in Sudan.

MILITARY RULE

In November 1958, the commander in chief of the army, Major General Ibrahim Abboud, took control of the government in a bloodless coup (overthrow). For the next six years, Abboud ran the country as he saw fit.

MAJOR GENERAL IBRAHIM

Abboud control of the government through a bloodless coup in 1958.

Abboud ended the political squabbling, but many of his decisions hurt the new nation. He aggravated relations with the south by appointing northerners to government posts in the south. Worse, he pursued a policy of encouraging Islam there. He established schools where all subjects were taught in Arabic, not English. Children attending these schools were required to adopt Arabic names. He also built mosques and prohibited Christian missionaries from opening new schools. The day of rest was changed from Sunday to Friday, in accordance with Islamic rather than Christian custom. When southerners objected to his actions, he accused the missionaries of provoking the protests and ordered all foreign missionaries expelled from the south.

Fearing religious persecution, non-Muslim southerners began fleeing to neighboring Uganda, Kenya, and Congo. In 1963 a guerilla army emerged in southern Sudan called the Anya-Nya (named for a poison made from snakes). Its attacks gained publicity for the opposition movement.

Abboud alienated another Sudanese minority by signing an agreement with Egypt to build a large dam across the Nile at Aswan in southern Egypt. The 364-foot-high (111-meter) dam would create a huge lake, 8 miles (13 km) across and more than 300 miles (483 km) long. The lake would drown Nubian villages and ancient monuments in northern Sudan. The government planned to move about fifty thousand Nubian farmers to a site in the desert of eastern Sudan, far from their homeland.

Nubians protested the plan, and sympathetic students and trade unionists joined in the protest. Abboud called out the army. His harsh suppression of the demonstrations created more opposition to his rule. In the end, the Nubians lost their land. Those that resettled in eastern Sudan met the resentment of local herders whose pasturelands were allotted to the Nubian farmers. Few prospered in their new location.

Strikes, riots, and protests finally unseated Abboud. In October 1964, huge crowds protested after a student was killed by police trying to stop an anti-government demonstration at the

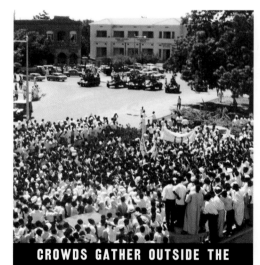

CROWDS GATHER OUTSIDE THE Presidential Palace in Khartoum during protests against the government in 1964.

University of Khartoum. Teachers, engineers, doctors, and lawyers joined trade unionists and civil servants in a general strike that brought cities across Sudan to a halt for several days. Twenty more civilians lost their lives in melees with the police before Abboud gave up. A transitional government replaced his regime. As the transitional government restored order and lifted censorship, Sudanese proudly celebrated their success at ousting the unpopular dictator.

In March 1965, the transitional government held a conference to try to resolve the southern issues. The results, however, were unsuccessful. Most northern politicians were ready to consider regional government for the south. But the southern politicians decided they wanted greater independence for the south, including southern control of finances, foreign affairs, and armed forces.

In preparation for the 1965 elections, the transitional government legalized political parties and made elections more democratic. For the first time, women were allowed to vote and run for office. The voting age was lowered to eighteen.

By that time, Omar al-Bashir was twenty-one. After independence, he had moved with his family to Khartoum, where he attended high school and worked part-time in an automotive garage. When he left high school, he chose a military career. As Sudan's second democratic government began, he was a student at the military college in Omdurman, across the Nile from Khartoum.

A CHANCE FOR DEMOCRACY

Because continuing rebel activity made the southern region unsafe, the 1965 elections in late April and early May were held only in the northern provinces. Twenty northerners ran unopposed for the southern seats in parliament. The Supreme Court ruled the election valid because the northerners were merchants who traded in the south and this fulfilled the residency requirements.

Even without the south, the new parliament represented a wide political spectrum. In addition to the two major parties (the Umma and the NUP), thirteen other parties vied for seats. Four parties made

PARLIAMENTARY GOVERNMENT

In a parliamentary system, instead of electing a president, voters choose members of parliament. The leader of the party that wins the most votes becomes the prime minister, who is the head of government (like the U.S. president). The prime minister appoints other members of parliament to form a cabinet, or group of advisers. Together the prime minister and the cabinet have executive power. Unlike the U.S. president, they are accountable to the parliament, not to the voters. In a multiparty democracy, if the leading party does not gain a majority in the election, the prime minister must form a coalition cabinet. In a coalition, two or more parties agree to work together to rule the country.

The prime minister may also act as the head of state, the chief public representative of the country. In some countries, the head of state has no political role but performs ceremonial duties assigned by the constitution. In the United Kingdom, for example, Queen Elizabeth II is the head small gains for minority points of view. The Sudan Communist Party elected eight members, among them Sudan's first woman member of parliament. Two regional parties gave the Beja and the Nuba a voice in the government. And a newly formed party called the Islamic Charter Front (ICF) brought militant Islamism into Sudanese politics. Led by Dr. Hassan al-Turabi, the head of the law faculty of the University of Khartoum, the ICF sought to establish a government based on Islam, in which religious laws would control all sectors of society.

As the front runner, the Umma Party chose their leader, Mohammed Ahmed Mahjoub, to be prime minister. The jockeying for power through coalitions resumed as Mahjoub formed his government.

The northern politicians agreed on one item: the "southern problem" should be solved militarily. "The only language southerners understand is force," Mahjoub declared. He sent his army south on a rampage. Soldiers destroyed homes, churches, fields, livestock, and even General Abboud's unpopular Arabic schools. They also committed many atrocities against civilians, especially in the towns of Juba and Wau, where they massacred hundreds in July 1965.

Even then southern politicians did not give up. They continued to campaign for recognition. By 1967 the southern provinces were at last somewhat calmer and southerners were allowed to vote for representatives in parliament. The rebel group Anya-Nya, however, remained in control of parts of the southern countryside.

That year Omar al-Bashir graduated from military college. He was not among the soldiers sent to the ongoing southern standoff. For the next two years, he served at the army's western headquarters at al-Fasher, then the capital of the province of Darfur.

The parliamentary government accomplished little during those two years. Peace was not achieved in the south and the constitution was left unwritten. The representatives of the political parties continued to spend most of their time vying for power.

In May 1969, a group of army officers, led by Colonel Gaafar al-Nimeiri, staged another coup. A Revolutionary Command Council replaced parliament and outlawed political parties. For the second time since independence, the military ruled Sudan.

A SECOND MILITARY REGIME

The May Revolution, as Nimeiri's coup was called, was swift and bloodless. But within a year, to maintain control, Nimeiri resorted to violent suppression of political protesters. In an air attack on Aba Island, his army killed thousands of Umma Party supporters. Among those slain was Al-Hadi ibn Abd al-Rahman, a grandson of the Mahdi, the religious leader of the Mahdiyya, the Mahdist brotherhood. The year after that, Nimeiri put down an attempted Communist Party coup and executed its leaders.

Officially voted president later that year, Nimeiri set about organizing Sudan. In 1972 he negotiated a cease-fire with southern rebels. He made the south a self-governing region

GAAFAR AL-NIMEIRI TOOK control of Sudan in a bloodless coup in 1969. He was elected president the next year.

with control of local government, education, public health, natural resources, and police. He increased local government throughout the country, ending the ethnic rule that had remained in many places.

To consolidate his power, Nimeiri created a new party, the Sudan Socialist Union, and declared it the sole legal political organization. He drafted a new constitution in 1973, making Sudan a "unitary, democratic, socialist and sovereign republic." It granted local self-government to the south and guaranteed religious freedom throughout Sudan. But it also established a presidential system in which Nimeiri wielded great authority as head of state. For example, as president, he could declare a state of emergency and suspend the constitution.

Peace in the south created the opportunity for young army officers such as Omar al-Bashir to expand their training abroad. The United States, Britain, Germany, and the Soviet Union (USSR) all had programs for foreign military personnel. Bashir trained as a paratrooper in the United States and in Cairo, Egypt. He was in Egypt in October 1973 when war broke out between Israel and Egypt. As second in command of a Sudanese airborne forces unit, he fought alongside Egyptian troops against Israel. He was later decorated by the Egyptian government for his service in that war. By then he was twenty-nine years old and moving steadily up the military ranks.

In the mid-1970s, Nimeiri launched major agricultural and industrial developments. He promoted the expansion of irrigated land and the addition of new cash crops, including peanuts and sugar. He planned for the construction of textile factories, sugar refineries, and a canal through the swamps of the Sudd. He also invited foreign companies to begin exploring for oil in Sudan.

Continued opposition and attempted coups, however, made it difficult for Nimeiri to lure investors to fund his schemes. The most serious threat was a failed coup in 1976. A coalition of Sudanese political parties, including the Umma, the NUP, and the Islamic Charter Front, attempted a coup with the help of Libya, Ethiopia, and the Soviet Union. More than one hundred people were executed for their supposed role in the plot. Nimeiri won a second national election in 1977, but his regime had been weakened.

Nimeiri had invested heavily in a huge bureaucracy and ambitious development schemes. These schemes had high costs and produced little income. The U.S. company Chevron discovered oil in south central Sudan in 1979. But it would be years before the industry could be sufficiently developed for Sudan to profit from it. Sudan's economy was rapidly deteriorating. Nimeiri wanted Sudan to qualify for loans from the International Monetary Fund (an organization of 185 countries that promotes economic development and provides temporary financial and technical assistance to its members). To meet the fund's requirements, Nimeiri reduced public spending, causing riots in the cities and famine in the countryside.

SHIFTING POLICIES

Meanwhile, Islamism—the movement for Islamic political and legal rule—was growing in popularity in Sudan, especially in the universities and the army. Although Nimeiri had at first taken a secular approach to government, in the late 1970s, he began to emphasize his Muslim religion. The change was either a personal conversion to a more fundamentalist Islam or a recognition that Islamist

ISLAMISM

Islamism, also referred to as "political Islam" and "Islamic fundamentalism," is a modern political movement. It aims to restructure government and society on the basis of Islam. The Islamists' goal is a society with no separation of religion and politics, where the religious principles of the Quran and the Sunna (the deeds and sayings of the prophet Muhammad) shape all facets of life.

politicians could help him remain in power. Either way, the Islamist political party, the Islamic Charter Front, was gaining many followers, and Nimeiri needed their support.

In a spirit of what he called National Reconciliation, Nimeiri asked politicians he had formerly opposed to serve in his cabinet. Among his appointments was Hassan al-Turabi, the leader of the Islamic Charter Front. Turabi became the minister of justice and attorney general.

Nimeiri began promoting Islamic social codes in 1980. He issued orders to government officials not to drink alcohol or gamble. In public appearances, he began wearing a traditional Arabic turban and *jellabiya*—a long white gown—instead of his military uniform. Newspapers carried photographs of him praying in a mosque.

In 1980 Omar al-Bashir entered the Military Staff College to earn a master of science degree. It is possible that he became involved in political Islam while he was there. He later said that the groundwork for the coup that would bring him to the presidency began during Nimeiri's regime. Referring to that time, he told an interviewer, "We began to group ourselves in total secrecy on the basis that we should be ready if and when there was a need to make our move to save the homeland."

In September 1983, as part of an Islamization program, Nimeiri declared a particularly harsh interpretation of Sharia (Islamic law) to be the law of the land. For a wide variety of crimes, severe punishments—such as floggings, amputations, and executions—replaced prison sentences. The laws applied to people of all religions.

The September Laws were especially opposed in southern Sudan. Nimeiri had already begun to curtail local rule in the south. He had also drawn a line around the area of Sudan that promised the greatest oil reserves to create a new state he called Unity. He had then declared Unity to be part of northern Sudan although it lay south of the border between north and south Sudan, a move that angered southern politicians. The imposition of Sharia was the last straw. Non-Muslim southerners objected to the extreme punishments of a religion they did not follow. After eleven years of peace, the civil war resumed.

The north was not much happier with the strict new laws. In January 1985, Mahmud Muhammad Taha, a seventy-six-year-old Muslim political leader, dared to speak out against them. Nimeiri promptly accused him of heresy (forbidden religious beliefs) and ordered him executed.

When Nimeiri left Khartoum in late March 1985 to visit Washington, D.C., people took to the streets to protest his rule. Unable to suppress the largest antigovernment demonstrations in Sudanese history, the army decided to "yield to the wishes of the people." Senior military officers took control of the country. Promising free, democratic elections after one year, the junta (a committee formed to govern a country temporarily during a period of unrest) announced that until then, a Transitional Military Council (TMC) would rule the country. Nimeiri did not return to Sudan but went into exile in Egypt.

SHARIA

Sharia is generally translated as "Islamic law," although it has the broader meaning of "justice," "rule of law," or even "way of life." It is not a system of laws but a framework or a set of guidelines for laws based on the sacred writings of Islam, the Quran, and the Sunna.

Sharia-derived laws are based on several schools of legal thought. One of these schools (the Maliki) was brought to Sudan by Arab jurists in the sixteenth century, during the Funj sultanate. Another (the Hanafi) was introduced in the nineteenth century during the Turkiyya. Both remain important in Sudanese law. The Mahdi rejected Funj and Turkish legal codes in favor of laws based on the strictest interpretation of the Quran and the Sunna, without the modifications and added interpretations of later Islamic scholars. As the divine leader, the Mahdi claimed power directly from God, which he declared gave him the right to interpret scripture and decree laws.

During the Anglo-Egyptian Condominium, the British replaced Islamic law with English civil law in all matters except for family and personal affairs of Muslims, such as marriage, divorce, and inheritance laws. When Sudan became an independent nation, the desire for a Sharia-based constitution was widespread among Sudanese Muslims. Non-Muslims opposed the idea, fearing they would not have the same legal rights as Muslims. This conflict contributed to the long delay in drafting a permanent constitution.

In 1972 the military dictator Gaafar al-Nimeiri drafted a secular (non-religious) constitution (which was ratified the following year). This move helped to end the first civil war (1955–1972). Eleven years later, however, his September Laws replaced the civil penal codes with the harsh punishments of a narrow, fundamentalist interpretation of Sharia. These included such punishments as public flogging for drinking alcohol, amputation of a hand for stealing, and execution for heresy. The enactment of these laws brought renewed rebellion in southern Sudan. The Bashir government has attempted to restore and extend this fundamentalist interpretation of Sharia to all facets of Sudanese society.

A THIRD SHOT AT DEMOCRACY

The TMC was true to its word. In April 1986, Sudanese citizens went to the polls for the first parliamentary elections in eighteen years. Not all Sudanese were able to vote, however. For security reasons, once again, no elections were held in the south, where the civil war was in progress.

The election gave the Umma Party ninety-nine seats in the parliament. The Democratic Unionist Party (DUP, formerly the National Unionist Party), came in second with sixty-six. The big surprise was the strong showing of the National Islamic Front (NIF, formerly the Islamic Charter Front). The newly named Islamist party came in a close third with fifty-two seats. Sadiq al-Mahdi, the Umma leader and a great grandson of the Mahdi, put together a coalition with the DUP. The DUP had always held views that differed from those of the Umma. Although both major parties grew out of Islamic religious sects, neither was comfortable with the stricter fundamentalist policies of the Islamists.

The new government inherited Nimeiri's economic disasters, the civil war in the south, and the unpopular Sharia laws. Without resources to expand the army, Sadiq decided to arm local militias known as *murahaliin* to fight the southern insurgents. Murahaliin were young cattle-herders in southwestern Sudan who guarded livestock as they moved between grazing areas. In dry periods, they had to compete with southern farmers for land and water. They were willing to fight in exchange for war booty. As paramilitary units with government weapons and support, they attacked southern civilians, looting their villages and stealing their cattle. They also burned their fields to make sure that those who escaped would not return.

of the government in Sudan after elections in 1986. He is the great-grandson of the Mahdi.

The war intensified, becoming increasingly savage and destructive. In spite of murahaliin terrorism, the Sudanese People's Liberation Army (SPLA), led by Col. John Garang, was gaining control of the south. The SPLA advanced into northern areas where many people opposed government policies.

Omar al-Bashir, meanwhile, had traveled to Malaysia, where he earned another master's degree. This one focused on counterinsurgency tactics (ways to combat uprisings). In 1987 he won a fellowship to the Sudan Academy of Administrative Sciences. The assignment once again put him in the capital, where he could be in close touch with political events. It is possible that he was involved with the National Islamic Front's growing influence in the army, but if there was any link, he kept it quiet at the time. The following year, Bashir was promoted to brigadier and put in charge of the 8th Brigade. His unit was sent to Southern Kordofan, where the SPLA was winning key victories. Bashir led a successful attack on the SPLA-held town of Mayoum, in oil-rich Unity State.

SADIQ FLIP-FLOPS

In November 1988, the DUP negotiated a peace agreement with the southern Sudanese People's Liberation Movement (SPLM, the political arm of the SPLA). Sadiq at first accepted the accord, even though a rival party had arranged it. Later, however, he rejected its terms because it called for an end to Nimeiri's September Laws until a constitutional conference could resolve the issue. The DUP left the Umma-DUP coalition in protest, and Sadiq formed a new alliance with the Islamist NIF even though he did not support their goal of an Islamist government for Sudan. Sadiq seemed to be only repeating Nimeiri's wheeling and dealing to stay in power.

In February 1989, the army high command presented Sadiq with an ultimatum demanding a commitment to end the war. Sadiq abandoned his new political allies and agreed to the DUP-SPLM peace protocol. By June 1989, the prospect for peace at last looked promising. Negotiations were scheduled to open in Ethiopia on July 1. In addition, a national constitutional conference, which would decide the question of Sharia in Sudan, was scheduled for September.

But Omar al-Bashir and a number of other junior officers of the Sudanese army did not want these issues to be resolved democratically. They had been preparing to overthrow the government if necessary to stop the peace process and create an Islamist government. On June 30, they carried out their well-planned coup and seized control of the government in Khartoum. The next day, Bashir emerged as the spokesperson of the group. From the beginning, however, Bashir clearly intended to be more than just the spokesperson for a junta. Whether or not he was the principal instigator or

> *"The present regime is the worst possible . . . until the next one."*
>
> —Sudanese saying

the mastermind of the coup, he was proud and ambitious. He took command and never looked back.

At the time, most Sudanese hoped that the Revolutionary Command Council for National Salvation, as the military junta called itself, would be another transitional government (as had occurred when Nimeiri was overthrown). They expected to have another chance at democracy. Yet it must have been hard to remain optimistic. In its short thirty-three years of independence, Sudan had already experienced twenty-four years of military rule. The vision of a democratic parliamentary republic that had driven the struggle for independence from British rule was fading fast. With a history that reaches back thousands of years, the Sudanese had lived only nine years free of authoritarian governments. It had been possible to overthrow Nimeiri. But Nimeiri with his Islamization agenda had paved the way for a much more brutal and extreme dictatorship that would be harder to dismantle.

CHAPTER 3

BASHIR'S

OMAR AL-BASHIR AND HIS FELLOW OFFICERS secretly planned a coup over many years. Senior officers apparently suspected Bashir's disloyalty to the government and in June of 1989 had ordered him out of the country to study. He was to attend an eighteen-month training course in Egypt, beginning July 1.

Bashir had only three weeks in Khartoum between leaving his garrison command in Southern Kordofan and reporting to the Nasser Military Academy in Cairo. As he prepared to leave for Egypt, a colleague joked, "It seems your coup will be postponed another year and a half."

But Bashir and his circle of conspirators were privately making all the final arrangements for the takeover. The coup began just hours before Bashir was to leave Khartoum. During the night, Bashir and his comrades, claiming they were under orders from senior

DICTATORSHIP

OMAR AL-BASHIR, SHOWN HERE in July 1989, and other officers in the Sudanese army took control of the government that year.

officers, took control of government buildings and army bases across Sudan.

On July 1, after the smoothly run, bloodless coup, Bashir introduced the new regime. Six brigadier generals, six colonels, two lieutenant colonels, and a major made up the Revolutionary Command Council for National Salvation, a name soon shortened to Revolutionary Command Council, or RCC. Few Sudanese knew who they were. Some but not all had ties to the Islamist NIF. Most came from the Nile Valley, but six were from other regions and ethnic groups. Three were southerners—a Dinka, a Shilluk, and a Zande. Two were Darfuri—one a Fur, the other a Berti—and one was a Nuba from Southern Kordofan. RCC members represented every branch of the armed forces—engineers, artillery, paratroops, signal corps, tank corps, infantry, air force, and navy. By choosing such a diverse group, the conspirators no doubt hoped to suggest that the coup had broader popular support than it did. One trait these men did seem to have had in common was loyalty to Bashir.

In his early broadcasts, Bashir said that no ideology (political philosophy) motivated the takeover. The coup intended only to rescue Sudan from Sadiq al-Mahdi, who had "failed the people" and "ruined the economy," he said. He called the coup a "revolution for the salvation of Sudan." It was a "revolution of the people against injustice, corruption, partisanship, and factionalism [small dissenting groups in government]." It was "not tilted to the right or left." His goal, he told reporters, was "to save the country from rotten political parties."

People tried to figure out who Bashir was and what his politics were. Some of Bashir's family members belonged to the Khatmiyya sect, the Islamic sect that was the political base of the DUP. One of Bashir's brothers had worked for a newspaper that supported the NIF. But Bashir declared that he opposed all partisan politics. "I do not belong to a religious party or to any non-religious party," he told an Egyptian journalist soon after the coup. "We, as officers, belong to the armed forces. Belonging to parties is not in our character; we have not worked inside parties."

Reporters noted that many RCC members were known to support Islamist policies. In response, Bashir devoted a whole issue of

Armed Forces, the only newspaper allowed after the coup, to denying that the junta had any links to the NIF.

SECURING CONTROL

Instead of presenting a political manifesto to explain the coup, Bashir focused on preventing a countercoup. He immediately dismissed senior commanders of the armed forces and assigned coup supporters to lead the air force, military intelligence, and the infantry school. Bashir appointed himself head of state, prime minister, defense minister, and commander in chief of the army. He also promoted himself to lieutenant general. During the first month of his regime, more than six hundred army officers and four hundred police officers received discharges.

Bashir also ordered the arrests of top government officials and political leaders. Sadiq al-Mahdi escaped arrest at first because he was attending a wedding the night of the coup. He hid out at a relative's home for a week, but Bashir's security forces found him and took him to Khartoum's Kobar Prison. The heads of the DUP and the NIF were already locked up there.

To silence other possible sources of dissent, Bashir dissolved parliament and banned all trade unions and political parties. By declaring a state of emergency, which Nimeiri's constitution allowed the head of government to do, Bashir gained control of all executive, legislative, and judicial power. To advise him, he named a twenty-one-member cabinet, sixteen of them civilians, but he did not make clear how much authority they would have in his administration. Many, but not all, of these advisers were actively involved in the NIF. Once again, a few southerners were included in the group, probably to mask the real purpose of the coup.

The ring of coup plotters, all members of the military, quickly established security forces. Among the key appointments was Bakri Hassan Salih, one of the coup plotters, to a special agency for internal security, the Bureau for the Security of the Revolution. A member of the paratrooper corps, like Bashir, Salih created an efficient and brutal secret police to suppress dissent. His agency arranged for private places to detain and interrogate political activists. It also recruited committees of citizens throughout Sudan to warn the government about dissenters and plans for subversive activities.

THE CIVIL WAR RESUMES

When Bashir took over, the cease-fire between the north and the south (which the Sadiq administration and the rebel SPLA had agreed on) was about to expire. After the coup, Bashir extended it. But although he claimed publicly to favor an end to the war, Bashir made no direct, formal contact with leaders of the SPLA or its political arm, the Sudanese People's Liberation Movement. People began to suspect that perhaps Bashir had extended the cease-fire only because it was the rainy season. In the rain-drenched south, many roads became impassable. It was not the best time for a military campaign.

In mid-July, Bashir announced that the conditions Sadiq had agreed to for peace negotiations would be scrapped. These conditions included the suspension of Islamic laws during the talks. Without publicly taking sides on the question of Sharia, Bashir suggested that the issue could be resolved by a national referendum.

Few Sudanese supported the idea of such a vote. Muslims who opposed the harsh punishments of Nimeiri's September Laws did not want to seem to vote against their religion. Non-Muslims, who were far outnumbered, saw no hope of the referendum going their way. Garang, the leader of the rebel SPLA (and SPLM), refused any compromise. He told interviewers, "We will accept total abolition [of Sharia] only." In the end, no referendum was held.

Meanwhile, the cease-fire was precarious. In July a land mine (a buried explosive set to explode when disturbed) injured a government soldier near the southern town of Wau. In response, his angry comrades attacked a camp of displaced southern civilians, who had come to Wau for protection. More than one hundred Dinkas lost their lives, and scores were badly injured. Neither the military nor Bashir's government investigated or even acknowledged the massacre.

In October more clashes erupted in southern Blue Nile State. Government planes also bombed villages in the Nuba Mountains, where the SPLA held several small enclaves.

As the rainy season came to an end, Bashir prepared for outright war. In November he decreed the Popular Defense Forces Law. This law legalized the ethnic militias that had already caused so much devastation in the south. It also created a voluntary Popular Defense Force (PDF), open to all Sudanese aged sixteen and over—except Dinka, the largest southern ethnic group. The PDF, it turned out, was not entirely voluntary. University students who did not volunteer risked losing their scholarships.

Former U.S. president Jimmy Carter made every effort to bring the two sides together for peace negotiations in Nairobi, Kenya. But by early December, it became clear that Bashir was determined not to give any ground on the issue of the Islamic laws. He gave the delegation he sent to the talks no authority to deal with that issue.

The SPLM was equally unwilling to give up the conditions they had agreed to with the previous government of Sudan. "We remain committed to . . . a Sudan in which religion is the individual's moral and personal law," the SPLM spokesperson declared. "We believe that religion cannot play a positive role in any state legislation."

The meeting broke off after five days. The pretense of peace negotiations over, the war escalated on both sides. Bashir (like Abboud earlier) believed he could solve the "southern problem" militarily.

BASHIR'S ISLAMISM

In August 1989, while the Sudanese and the outside world were still trying to figure out the new dictator, Bashir traveled to Tehran, the capital of Iran, to meet with Iranian leaders. In 1979 Islamists had overthrown the shah (ruler) of Iran, Mohammad Reza Pahlavi, and established an Islamist government. Most Iranian Muslims are of the Shia sect, and most Sudanese Muslims are of the Sunni sect. But a mutual interest in political Islam as a revolutionary movement seems to have outweighed the religious differences. At the time, Bashir kept this diplomatic journey secret, in order not to reveal the Islamist goals of his coup.

Close observers of the political scene in Sudan noticed that some members of the RCC openly supported Islamist politics, as did many of the civilians appointed to the cabinet. Rumors also circulated that although Hassan al-Turabi, the NIF party chairperson, was a political prisoner, he received better treatment than the other prisoners. He had been allowed to return home to pack a suitcase when he was arrested and to receive visits in prison from party members.

> *"Sudanese are very talkative. As a people we like to discuss freely. We don't like to be told when to go home at night. Now many people don't want to talk at all. It's dangerous. Nobody knows yet what these fellows [Bashir and other coup members] are really up to."*
>
> —Khartoum intellectual to a *Washington Post* reporter, mid-July 1989

At the end of November, Turabi was freed from Kobar Prison and assigned to house arrest, while Sadiq al-Mahdi remained in prison several months longer. The failure of the peace talks in early December led the RCC to declare on December 7 that the September Laws, suspended during the peace talks, would once more be imposed.

Any doubts that remained about Bashir's Islamist views vanished the following April. Twenty-eight army officers, among them several who had pressured Sadiq al-Mahdi a year earlier to negotiate with the SPLM, were accused of plotting to overthrow Bashir. After a trial that lasted only two hours, they were executed. They wanted to "abolish Islamic law," Bashir explained, adding, "There can be no secular government in Sudan."

Two of Bashir's coconspirators on the RCC spoke out against the execution of the officers. Bashir quickly removed them from the RCC and their government posts. Although both had played important roles in the coup, neither man belonged to the NIF. Since Bashir was no longer hiding the Islamist purpose of the coup, he could afford to let them go. The Dinka member also objected to the execution and asked to resign. But Bashir kept him on the RCC for another year, probably because, as a southerner, he was still politically useful.

THE NIF REGIME

As Sudan became an openly Islamist state, Hassan al-Turabi returned to NIF politics. He held no official post in the government but was active behind the scenes. Freed from house arrest, he traveled the globe praising Bashir's Sudan. A skillful speaker with an engaging personality, Turabi painted glowing pictures of Sudan as an Islamic republic, "governing with justice and equity and open to all sections and classes of society." "The difference between a democracy and an Islamic state," he explained, "would only be that there is a higher system of law on top of all institutions of government, which is the Sharia."

Turabi remained the leader of the NIF party. Like the other political parties, the NIF was officially banned, but in fact, it was slowly gaining control of Sudan. The government fired heads of Sudanese universities and replaced them with members of the NIF. Army officers who were NIF supporters won promotions. Those who were not were dismissed. Security was entrusted to NIF activists.

The government began to require that all government employees and students undergo three months of training for the PDF militias. Prayers and religious lectures alternated with military drills and boot camp discipline. "They wash our brains," said one young student. Daily chanting of slogans identified the SPLA, the United States, Russia, Britain, and France as enemies of Sudan. The purpose of PDF training, Bashir said in a speech, was "to reshape the Muslim Sudanese citizen."

Political analysts began referring to the government of Sudan as the NIF regime. Many people were still not certain whether the NIF had been involved in the coup from the start or whether the Islamists had somehow gained power afterward. Some wondered if Bashir was really the head of the government or just a puppet whose strings were being pulled by Hassan al-Turabi. If Bashir was only a figurehead, some predicted, his days as dictator of Sudan were numbered.

As the NIF connection grew clearer, the party eliminated some government officials who had collaborated with the coup but were not members of the NIF. These people had been given positions on the RCC and the cabinet in order to hide the NIF's role in the coup. Some of these former collaborators went into exile and spoke out publicly against the regime. They revealed that a shadowy Council of the Defenders of the Revolution (also

> "Omar al-Bashir is me. . . . He represents my aspirations and those of the Sudanese people for an Islamic state, governing with justice and equity and open to all sections and classes of society."
> —Hassan al-Turabi, 1994 interview in Khartoum

referred to as the Council of Forty) was really running Sudan. Part military and part civilian, the group met at night at a mosque in Khartoum.

The leaders of this council were NIF chairperson Hassan al-Turabi and his deputy chairperson, Ali Osman Muhammad Taha. "I advise our politicians, who want to rule Sudan on the basis of Islamic principles," Turabi told a Swiss reporter in 1994. "I do my best so that the Islamic movement fully permeates our society." Turabi's main concern was with ideology and spreading Islamism around the world. Taha took care of the details of enforcing Islamism in Sudan. A longtime friend of Bashir, Taha had acted as liaison between the NIF and the army before the coup. Often credited with masterminding the takeover, he was perhaps the most powerful member of the regime.

Within the various governing units—the RCC, the cabinet, and the Council of

ALI OSMAN MUHAMMAD TAHA attends an Arab League conference in 1995. Taha is one of the most powerful members of Bashir's regime.

Forty—which had overlapping memberships and no constitutional basis, the chains of command and areas of responsibility were not always clear. One ousted minister told a journalist that Colonel al-Taiyib Ibrahim, the minister for cabinet affairs, "oftentimes countermanded the orders of al-Bashir or issued orders in the name of al-Bashir without the latter's knowledge." Who was running Sudan?

PRESIDENT BASHIR

If NIF leaders Turabi and Taha were the real powers behind the throne, Bashir still managed to hold onto his public role as the Sudanese head of government and head of state. Even with his many loyal supporters on the junta, Bashir had to be cautious. He could not act entirely on his own, but he was not willing to be a puppet. So long as he continued to be the principal spokesperson for the RCC, he knew how to take advantage of his public position. For one thing, he was savvy about publicity. Soon after the coup, when the NIF organized rallies that attracted few people, Bashir put his foot down: no more rallies. He was not going to let himself be humiliated. Meanwhile, he played the role of decider, issuing the decrees that the NIF prepared.

In 1992 Bashir appointed the Transitional National Assembly to act as the legislative branch of government until a new constitution could be drafted and elections held. This assembly was intended to be part of a change from military government to a civilian government. In October 1993, Bashir dissolved the RCC and declared himself the president of Sudan.

A new governing organization gradually developed through Bashir's presidential decrees. One decree divided the country into twenty-six states. This division broke up long-established regions, such as Darfur, into smaller, easier-to-control areas. The government in Khartoum appointed the governors of these states. In December 1995, Bashir decreed elections for the new National Assembly and the president of the republic to be held in March 1996.

With the ban on opposition parties, a huge field of forty-two presidential candidates ran against President Bashir. The government allowed the little-known candidates only twelve days to campaign for office. Official sources reported that Bashir was elected with 75.7 percent of the vote. "We have fully returned power in full to the people," he declared after his landslide victory. Former Sudanese leaders, in exile abroad, denounced the vote as a sham.

The NIF won almost all the seats in the assembly. That was hardly surprising. Of the 400 seats, 125 were filled by appointed officials before the elections and 50 were reserved for NIF stalwarts. More than a thousand candidates vied for the remaining 225 seats, but NIF supporters in every district made certain that voter registration lists and ballot boxes went missing in areas with

OMAR AL-BASHIR ADDRESSES the media after winning the presidential election in March 1996.

> "At first this Government was popular, but after one or two years it lost most of its popularity because they used the Islamic religion very badly."
>
> —Siddiq Sidahmed Hassan, forty-nine-year-old Muslim shopkeeper in Khartoum, March 1996

strong non-NIF candidates. Hassan al-Turabi was among the victors in the elections. Taking his first official role in the regime, he became the speaker of the newly elected assembly. The assembly set to work drafting a new Islamist constitution for Sudan.

In a May 1998 referendum, 96.7 percent of the Sudanese who voted approved the new constitution. President Bashir signed it in a public ceremony on June 30, the ninth anniversary of his coup. The constitution settled the question of Sharia—which became the sole source of legislation in Sudan—and increased the powers of the presidency.

Confident of his power, Bashir invited Sudanese politicians in exile to return to Sudan and take part in the political freedom the new constitution guaranteed. In November the National Assembly formally ended the ban on political parties, and in early 1999, several parties registered. In 2000 Sadiq al-Mahdi returned to Sudan from self-imposed exile and resumed leadership of the Umma Party. Some other politicians, however, held back because they felt the conditions were still too restrictive. To register, parties—now called "alliances," a name somehow considered less partisan than "parties"—had to swear their support for the constitution. Not every political group was comfortable giving allegiance to Islamic law.

WAR IN THE SOUTH

During the years that Bashir was establishing his regime in Khartoum, the civil war raged on in the south. The first winter after the coup, Bashir's army and the newly recruited Popular Defense Force found themselves up against a well-organized offensive by the SPLA. The war was not going to be as easily won as Bashir imagined. The resulting devastation, made worse by drought, prompted the international community to continue to press hard for dialogue between the two sides.

In the early 1990s, the Organization of African Unity (OAU), a confederation of fifty-three African countries, arranged for talks in Abuja, the capital of Nigeria. Before the talks began, however, the SPLM split into two factions. One wanted complete independence for southern Sudan. The other wanted a unified Sudan that would be set up as a confederation with separate governments for north and south. To make negotiations possible, the two SPLM factions agreed to ask for "self-determination" for the south. The term was deliberately vague. The idea was simply that southerners would have some choices that would be spelled out later. Afraid southerners would vote for independence, the government of Sudan refused to consider the idea.

The fighting between the two southern factions was helping the north. Bashir had no interest in talking about peace when northern forces were gaining territory. The southern rebels had also lost important support from neighboring Ethiopia, where a regime change occurred in May 1991. Bashir's army and PDF militias, working in tandem, developed ruthless tactics of bombing, raiding, and looting civilian villages and farms. The combined forces successfully depopulated large areas. People and livestock were killed or

CHILDREN RUN FROM A DESTROYED IDP CAMP IN THE NUBA MOUNTAINS

in central Sudan. The Sudanese government bulldozed part of the camp in 1996. The people in the camp had lost their homes owing to war in the area.

abducted. Survivors fled to city slums or to camps for what relief agencies call "internally displaced persons" (IDPs). Even these grim places of refuge were not always safe from attack. In addition to gaining ground in the south, government troops attacked pockets of resistance in the Nuba Mountains.

When a second round of talks in Abuja took place in 1993, the southern factions proposed a confederation. But Bashir also rejected that condition. He still thought he could win the war and create an Islamist nation.

One reason for Bashir's confidence was Sudan's growing oil industry, which assisted the north's war effort both financially and logistically. During the 1990s, four companies based in China, Malaysia, Canada, and Sudan formed the Greater Nile Petroleum Operating Company (GNPOC). They built a 994-mile (1,600 km) pipeline capable of carrying 250,000 barrels of oil a day to Port Sudan on the Red Sea. The pipeline delivered its first crude oil to petroleum tankers in

August 1999. By 2001 oil revenues were funding 40 percent of Bashir's government. Much of the money went to the war.

The cost to the southern Sudanese was staggering. Airstrips built for oil operations became convenient air bases for military strikes against southern forces. Roads intended for moving oil trucks and rigs facilitated the movement of government troops. Civilians living in oil producing areas were forced to relocate, usually to shabby IDP camps that provided no means of livelihood and were vulnerable to military attack.

The means used to relocate civilians were brutal. A Nuer man in an IDP camp described how bombers and helicopter gunships attacked his village for two hours every other morning over a two-week period, shooting at cattle, goats, adults, and children: "They fired guns—they open the door and shoot from machine guns—flying very low. They would target living things. . . . We would have died if we had stayed." Once people fled, the enemy destroyed their homes, their crops, and any belongings they left behind to make certain they did not return.

BASHIR VS. TURABI

The slight opening of the government to more democratic procedures in 1998 and 1999 increased a rift between Turabi and Bashir. First, Turabi reorganized the NIF into a new "political alliance" with the name National Congress Party (NCP). Turabi then changed the leadership rules of the party to increase his control of it and reduce that of Bashir. He was able to do this because he had a larger following within the party than Bashir did. Bashir's main support came from the army.

These changes meant that although Bashir would be the NCP candidate for president in the next elections, Turabi would be choosing his vice presidents, cabinet members, and senior government officials.

Then, as speaker of the assembly, Turabi began proposing amendments to the constitution that further reduced Bashir's power as president. One amendment was to allow a two-thirds vote of the assembly to remove the president. Another was to create a directly elected prime minister (a role Bashir previously took as part of his presidency). A third was to give citizens the right to elect regional governors.

In December 1999, two days before the assembly was slated to vote on these measures, Bashir took action. Declaring a state of emergency, he ordered the army to surround the legislative building with tanks. He then dismissed Turabi as speaker of the assembly and declared the assembly dissolved. He promptly reorganized his cabinet to ensure all its members supported his regime.

As Bashir's five-year term drew to an end, Turabi called for a boycott of the upcoming elections. Using his emergency powers, Bashir removed him as head of the National Congress Party and named himself party chief. In response, Turabi formed an opposition party, the Popular National Congress Party (PNCP). Other parties, among them the Umma Party, joined the PNCP boycott of the election. Once again, Bashir "won"—this time with 86.5 percent of the vote. Members of his National Congress Party, who ran unopposed, filled the assembly. Voter turnout was small, but Bashir cheerfully noted as he cast his ballot that the right to boycott was "part of the freedom" Sudanese citizens enjoyed.

In his inaugural speech in February 2001, Bashir appeared less jovial. Dressed in full military uniform and wearing dark glasses, he declared that to achieve a strong government it might be necessary to restrain challengers intent on seizing power. He had already exercised that authority by extending the state of emergency to the end of 2001.

Two weeks after being sworn in, Bashir ordered the arrest of Hassan al-Turabi and thirty members of the NCP for "conspiring with the rebels to topple the government." Turabi's alleged conspiracy took place at a meeting with SPLM leader Garang in Geneva, Switzerland. There the two Sudanese leaders signed a "memorandum of understanding" to promote joint "peaceful resistance" to the Bashir regime. When he returned to Khartoum, Turabi held a press conference calling on the Sudanese to protest Omar al-Bashir's regime. Well aware that demonstrations and strikes by civilians had deposed earlier dictators in Sudan, Bashir was not ready to risk his own overthrow. Turabi remained in prison for the next thirty-two months.

THE LONG ROAD TO PEACE

The international community did not give up trying to end Sudan's civil war. During the 1990s, the Intergovernmental Authority for Drought and Development (IGADD), a regional organization of Sudan, Djibouti, Eritrea, Ethiopia, Kenya, Somalia, and Uganda stepped in. It had originally formed to address problems of desertification (expanding desert) in the Sahel. The government of Sudan agreed to meet with IGADD out of respect for "neighborly and brotherly relations."

Getting the two sides to a point where they could agree on ways of approaching the problems took several years. IGADD became so involved with the issue that it dropped the *D* for "Drought" and became IGAD. Its members felt that conflict management was essential for development to occur. The United States, Norway, Italy, Canada, Britain, and Australia declared themselves friends of IGAD to support the peace process.

Slowly the pressure paid off. For Bashir, it was perhaps the need for international respectability that softened his resistance. He also had new battles to fight against unemployment and discontent in northern Sudan, a huge debt, and the hostility of his old ally Turabi. Even the newly tapped oil money was vanishing into the black hole of war. Actual peace talks had finally begun in Nairobi, Kenya, in January 2000. By 2002 the government of Sudan and the SPLM were establishing procedures for achieving peace.

In July, leaders signed the Machakos Protocol, an agreement reached in Machakos, a town near Nairobi. The agreement provided for a six-year transitional government leading to a referendum in which southerners could vote on southern independence. Peace seemed close even though more discussion was needed on issues such as wealth sharing. But within a short time, the momentum for peace slowed. Another conflict was erupting in Sudan.

REBELLION IN DARFUR

The war that broke out in Darfur in 2003 was in many ways similar to the conflict in southern Sudan. In both regions, people were rebelling against a government in Khartoum that had neglected their needs, given them little role in government, and looked down on them as culturally inferior.

Darfur had other problems as well. Repeated droughts had heightened competition between herders and farmers over scarce water and pastureland. Conflicts over land and water had once been solved by negotiations between ethnic leaders. But since the 1960s, rebels from neighboring Chad and Libya had used Darfur as a staging area to prepare attacks against the Chadian and Libyan governments. Weapons and ammunition became easily available. For little more than the price of a goat, Darfuris could purchase a Kalashnikov assault rifle at a local market. To some Darfuris, guns seemed simpler than negotiation as a way to solve land conflicts.

THE BLACK BOOK

In May 2000, some NIF supporters from Darfur who had sided with Turabi in his quarrel with Bashir decided to publicize Bashir's neglect of the region. Calling themselves Seekers of Truth and Justice, they published the *Black Book: Imbalance of Power and Wealth in the Sudan*. This tract presented detailed information concerning how the government in Khartoum ignored Darfur and other outlying regions of Sudan. Listing specific ethnic groups, it showed that members of the Nile Valley elite had dominated Sudan's government since independence. Three groups—the Jaaliyyin, the Shayqiyya, and the Danaqla—representing 5.4 percent of the population of Sudan had supplied its presidents, generals, judges, parliamentary leaders, and the heads of government banks and development schemes. These elite groups also held posts at every level of the Sudanese bureaucracy. The people of Darfur were already aware of the general ideas of the book, but the publication of so many specific details no doubt helped to fire up the revolt in Darfur.

KALASH

In the 1990s, Kalashnikov rifles (Russian-designed assault rifles) were so easy to come by that they replaced swords as the weapons of choice among Darfuri bandits. "The Kalash brings cash," went a popular rhyme. "Without Kalash, you're trash."

Adding to the violence in Darfur were ideas of Arab supremacy spread by such leaders as Muammar al-Qaddafi, the military dictator of Libya. Pro-Arab propaganda encouraged violence against non-Arab ethnic groups. These ideas helped split Darfur into Arab and non-Arab factions.

Bashir did not help this situation. Since the beginning of his regime, he had appointed governors who favored Arab ethnic groups, such as the Rizeigat, the Beni Halba, and the Missiriyya, over African groups, such as the Fur, the Zaghawa, and the Masalit. When Bashir divided Darfur into three states in 1993, the new state lines cut through Fur homelands, so that the majority ethnic group in the region became a minority group in each new state. In 2000 he appointed a governor who replaced all ethnic African police (who made up 80 percent of the force) with Arab militias.

In 2002 Fur, Masalit, and Zaghawa activists in Darfur formed a rebel group, the Sudanese Liberation Movement/Army (SLM/A)— not to be confused with the south's SPLM/A—and began to raid army garrisons in remote areas of Darfur. A different opposition group, the Justice and Equality Movement (JEM) also formed. It was led by Darfuris who had supported the Islamist regime but had sided with Turabi, not Bashir. The two groups had little in common. But in April

TOYOTA WARFARE

In the 1980s, when Libya tried to seize northern Chad, the Chadian army developed a new weapon—Toyota Land Cruisers. First, they sawed off the roof of the car so that troops could jump in and out more easily. Then they mounted machine guns and automatic cannons on the vehicle. Chadian forces were able to attack more swiftly and turn more easily with these improvised weapons, called technicals, than the invading Libyan army with their heavy tanks. Technicals have proven valuable in the trackless deserts of Darfur, where both sides use them in the conflict.

2003, they joined forces and staged a surprise predawn attack on the military air base in al-Fasher, the capital of Northern Darfur.

The strike was successful. By noon the rebels had destroyed four bombers and gunships, seized military supplies, killed seventy-five soldiers and officers, and captured thirty-two, among them the base commander. Only nine rebels lost their lives in the raid. The rebels' bold move attracted recruits to their cause. Other successful raids followed, and the conflict spread into Southern Darfur.

BASHIR STRIKES BACK

Bashir was quick to retaliate. Using the same strategies they had developed in southern Sudan and the Nuba Mountains, military units and militias worked together to terrorize ethnic groups suspected of sympathizing with the rebels. Instead of fighting the rebels, they attacked civilians.

To strengthen its Popular Defense Force, the government recruited the private Arab militias that already existed in Darfur. This strategy pitched two groups of Darfuris against each other. It created a civil war in Darfur between Arabic culture groups who sided with the government and the African culture groups who did not.

In Darfur the principal military targets were often poor people not involved in the rebellion. Some were farmers living in small villages, growing millet (a grain used for food) and raising a few goats. Others herded sheep, cattle, or camels over long distances to seasonal pastures. Attacks generally began early in the morning. Victims would awake to the roar of bombers or helicopter gunships. After bombing or strafing the village or camp, the air force flew off, and the militias moved in on horseback or camelback. People called the militias *janjawiid*, meaning "devil-riders," in Arabic, a term used earlier for bandits. The janjawiid would kill men in front of their wives and children, rape women, loot houses and set them afire, and kill livestock or herd them away. The janjawiid stuffed wells with bodies to pollute the water supply and burned storehouses and fields. This "scorched earth" policy (a tactic intended to make the land uninhabitable) was directed mainly at the Fur, Masalit, and Zaghawa ethnic groups.

The government of Sudan tried to prevent news of the war from spreading, but a few Darfuris managed to escape the violence and flee abroad. Foreign reporters, hearing about their experiences, sneaked across the Chadian border to film the devastation. People and organizations around the world reacted in horror. They soon asked whether the Sudanese government was committing ethnic cleansing (driving an ethnic group away from its homeland) or genocide. Genocide, according to the United Nations, means "acts committed with the intent to destroy, in whole or in part, a national, ethnic, racial or religious group."

President Bashir defended his regime by saying that he had no control over the violence of the janjawiid. He denied any involvement of government troops in their activities. The government publication *SudaNews* claimed that international reports on Darfur were "sensationalist and disproportionate."

PEACE IN THE SOUTH

As the crisis worsened in Darfur, the talks in Kenya to bring peace to southern Sudan were taking longer than anyone had imagined. Some outside observers suspected that the government of Sudan was simply stalling for time, wanting to crush the rebellion in Darfur before establishing the transitional government called for in the Machakos Protocol. The steps involved were not easy ones for Bashir. He was not eager to let go of any part of Sudan's wealth and governmental power, much less share them with a long-term enemy.

Finally, two and a half years after signing the protocols for the peace agreement, the Comprehensive Peace Agreement was ready. It called for merging armed forces, sharing oil wealth and other resources, and dividing government posts during the six-year transition period. Omar al-Bashir was to remain the president of Sudan, with John Garang as the vice president. A census was to be completed by 2007 and elections held in 2009. At the end of six years, in 2011, southern states would vote on whether to remain part of Sudan or become an independent nation.

The Comprehensive Peace Agreement represents a major milestone in Sudanese history. Not only has it brought two decades of civil war to an end, it provides a blueprint for building a democratic nation. Its unusual provision for two governments joined by an overarching Government of National Unity has resolved the difficult problem of Sharia law by allowing it to be imposed in the north while the south remains secular. This solution may not work over the long term, but it has brought hope to southern Sudan.

The two sides signed the agreement in a formal ceremony on January 9, 2005, in Nairobi. Thousands of onlookers crowded into the sports stadium where the ceremony was held. Most were Sudanese refugees. They cheered joyfully as leaders signed the agreement. "I hope my children don't have to be refugees like I was," said Grace Datiro, who had fled Sudan as a teenager, twenty-two years earlier. "I pray that this fighting is over forever and that we can finally live in peace." Casting a shadow on the celebration, however, was growing international awareness of the ongoing violence in Darfur.

NO PEACE IN DARFUR

Bashir's lies about Darfur were not deflecting international criticism. In January 2006 and again in January 2007, the African Union (AU), which had replaced the OAU in 2002, rejected his bid for the presidency of that organization. It was not just his fellow Africans who were putting pressure on Bashir. The United Nations, the United States, the European Union (EU), and the Arab League were pushing for a peace settlement in Darfur and setting deadlines that kept being extended. At peace talks in Abuja, Nigeria, mediators worked with both sides. They also tried to get the various rebel groups to agree on their demands. The SLM had split into two factions that disagreed on many issues. The JEM had its own agenda for peace.

During the negotiations, the African Union took on the job of monitoring cease-fire agreements, but the AU troops, which grew to seven thousand by the end of 2005, could not stop the violence.

Finally, on May 5, 2006, Bashir and Minni Minnawi, the leader of one faction of the SLM/A, signed the Darfur Peace Agreement. Unfortunately, that did not end the fighting. The AU lacked the troops and equipment to bring security to Darfur and looked to hand that responsibility over to the United Nations. But Bashir was determined not to allow UN forces into Darfur. In September 2006, he traveled to New York to tell the United Nations General Assembly meeting, "We categorically and totally reject the transformation of the African Union Forces in Darfur to a UN force." Only in December 2007 was an AU-UN joint force (known as UNAMID) finally allowed to begin operations in Darfur. In September 2008, 10,461 UNAMID personnel arrived to protect civilians, ease humanitarian access, promote rule of law, and help to implement the provisions of the peace agreement.

In spite of these efforts, peace remains elusive. By mid-2008, the estimated numbers of displaced Darfuris in Sudan had risen to 2.4 million and the number killed to between 200,000 and 400,000. Owing to the chaotic conditions in Darfur, more precise numbers for casualties were not available. The government of Sudan, for example, put the number of Darfuris killed at 10,000. Many other Darfuris had fled to Chad, where relief agencies calculated 250,000 were living in refugee camps.

On July 14, 2008, Luis Moreno-Ocampo, the prosecutor of the International Criminal Court (ICC), asked the judges to issue an arrest warrant for Omar Hassan al-Bashir on charges of murder, crimes against humanity, and genocide in Darfur. On the day of the announcement, demonstrators in Khartoum (among them civil servants threatened with loss of their jobs if they did not attend) protested the war crimes case. Bashir then traveled to Darfur, where he appeared at pep rallies in each of the three Darfuri capitals, al-Fasher, Nyala, and Geneina. He promised to drill water wells, build schools, and reach out to rebel groups. "We are with you, Darfur!" he declared. He praised the AU and UN peacekeepers that he had so long opposed. Then in spite of the sweltering heat, he danced around cheerfully waving his cane, secure, unafraid, and convinced of his innocence.

When the judges issued a warrant for Bashir's arrest in March 2009, however, he lashed back angrily. Saying the ICC could "eat" the warrant, he ordered foreign aid agencies out of Sudan. These organizations were providing food, water, shelter, sanitation, education, and medical care to millions of Darfuris driven from their homes by government troops and militias. Then he showed off his military might. Armored personnel carriers, technicals mounted with heavy machine guns and anti-aircraft guns, and 150 military trucks crammed with armed soldiers paraded through al-Fasher while two Chinese-made ground-attack planes zoomed low overhead. The message was clear: Bashir had no intention of stepping down or surrendering.

CHAPTER 4

LIVING IN

BEFORE OMAR AL-BASHIR'S COUP, Sudanese citizens enjoyed many freedoms. They could run for office and vote in elections, speak out against the government, read a wide array of newspapers reflecting many different political points of view, publish editorials accusing government officials of corruption, hold demonstrations to protest rising prices, and agitate for higher wages or better working conditions.

When the coup occurred on June 30, 1989, they lost every one of those freedoms. But Sudan's democratically elected leaders had proved so incompetent that many Sudanese welcomed the abrupt change in government. Military rule, they hoped, would end the war, bring down prices, and restore order. Then new elections could be held. Within weeks of the coup, however, Sudanese citizens realized that the National Salvation Revolution had no intention of restoring democracy to Sudan.

BASHIR'S SUDAN

Immediately after the coup, military and police patrols stood guard around the cities of northern Sudan. Daily life was reasonably calm, though lines for food and gasoline were no shorter than before. Newspapers had disappeared, and radio broadcasts announced new government regulations, such as an 11 P.M. to 4 A.M. curfew.

As the summer wore on, the Sudanese became more aware of the seriousness of the coup. In August eight presidents of trade unions petitioned for the return of their unions' assets and permission to resume regular union activities. No previous dictator in Sudan had suppressed trade unions. But the RCC immediately arrested the union leaders and jailed them on charges of opposing the government. A month later, the RCC published a list of ninety doctors it proposed to dismiss. After the junta fired the first

> *"We have never known a situation like this in our history. Today you are frightened to ask your brother if he is in the NIF [National Islamic Front]."*
>
> —a prominent Sudanese opposition figure
> (unnamed for fear of arrest), 1993

fifteen, other doctors went on strike in protest. Security forces promptly arrested the striking doctors. The president of the doctors' union was sentenced to death and the union's secretary to fifteen years' imprisonment. To those horrified by the death sentence, Bashir replied, "Anyone who betrays this nation does not deserve the honor of living."

Stories of atrocities and a list of jailed politicians, civil servants, labor leaders, and southerners began to circulate in Khartoum. The International Arab Bar Association, the Catholic Church, and the International Labour Organization were among the first to speak out against the mass arrests, detentions without charges, and torture of detainees. Some interrogations, they reported, were so brutal that those being questioned died.

A secret Human Rights Committee for Sudan collected information and published its first report in commemoration of UN Human Rights Day, which is celebrated annually on December 10. By the end of the year, at least 150 lawyers, trade union leaders, and university professors were being held in jail without charges. Two businessmen had been sentenced to death and executed for using foreign currency. The RCC's severe measures shocked the Sudanese.

HUMAN RIGHTS IN SUDAN

Frequent reports by Africa Watch, Amnesty International, Human Rights Watch, the United Nations Human Rights Commission, the United States Department of State Country Reports on Human Rights and other human rights organizations have traced a continuous pattern of human rights violations by the Bashir regime. In response to accusations, Foreign Minister Hussein Suleiman Abu Salih told U. S. ambassador Donald Petterson in 1993, "The government of Sudan will never accept outside political pressures designed to make Sudan get down on its knees." None of the reports were true, he declared. "There is a conspiracy against Sudan."

Since 1993 the UN Human Rights Commission has appointed a series of special rapporteurs (investigators who report to the UN on human rights) to look into Sudan. All their reports, most of them highly critical, have helped keep the world informed, blocked some of Bashir's worst crimes, and opened the way for humanitarian aid to reach his victims.

According to special rapporteur Sima Simar's report in September 2008, Sudan's human rights conditions are again growing worse. Especially in Darfur, she noted "much more aerial bombardment and ground attack" on civilians than the previous year and far less access to humanitarian services. Army attacks on relief workers and their convoys are the sole reason aid cannot reach displaced civilians in Darfur.

Bashir, meanwhile, is pressuring the UN to abolish the mandate for a special rapporteur. The Sudanese government should be allowed to establish its own Human Rights Commission, he argues. He promises the commission will closely watch the situation in the country.

No previous Sudanese dictator had committed so many human rights violations. Bashir did not mince words: "The revolution will destroy anyone who stands in the way," he told a NIF rally, "and amputate those who betray the nation."

MORALITY POLICE

As Bashir made the Islamist agenda of the coup more evident, the new regime began to change Sudanese social life to conform to fundamentalist religious practice. Drinking alcohol was forbidden. Men and women were ordered not to dance in each other's presence, even at family weddings. Used to enjoying life, most Sudanese at first ignored the bans—until police armed with batons, tear gas, and guns burst in to break up parties, arresting everyone, even children.

Women were especially affected by the new regime. The government attempted to enforce what Sudanese women wore in public. Long black, gray, or white dresses were supposed to cover everything except their hands. A matching hijab, or veil, was to hide hair, neck, and ears. Some Sudanese Muslim women dressed this way before, but it was voluntary.

"They are turning us Muslims against Islam."
—Sudanese professional woman commenting on the Bashir regime, 1992

FEMALE STUDENTS FROM AL-AZHARI UNIVERSITY IN KHARTOUM WALK home from class in 2007. Under Bashir's regime, women have been required to adopt long dresses and head coverings.

Not all Sudanese women adopted the dress code. Many preferred Western styles of clothing or the traditional Sudanese *tobe*, a colorful fabric wrapped loosely around the body from head to foot. "How you dress—I consider this a basic human right, as much as what you say and what you think," said a university administrator. But even in tobes, some women were arrested and publicly flogged for not covering their hair.

It was not just clothing that limited women's lives. Before the Bashir regime, many Sudanese women worked outside the home as teachers, doctors, lawyers, and judges. Now they found their professional lives in jeopardy. The ideal Sudanese woman, Bashir declared, "should take care of herself, her children, her home, her reputation, and her husband." If she had no children and her family needed her income, a woman could teach, take care of children, or provide health care to children and other women.

Several new laws made it difficult for women to work outside the home. Women were told they could no longer work in cafés or alongside men in offices. They were also not allowed to go out after dark or to travel out of the country without a male companion. In the years after the coup, the number of women working in government offices dropped noticeably. The government fired the woman who was dean of the college of nursing at the University of Khartoum and replaced her with a man. Poor women who sold tea on the streets in the evenings lost their meager income.

The mood became anxious as the regime's security forces arrested more and more people. Some were jailed for violating the curfew or other restrictions imposed by the regime. But many more were arrested at home, late at night, for no apparent reason. The government detained hundreds of politicians, trade unionists, students, professionals, military officers, and religious leaders. Many were tortured and some executed with only brief military trials. "We're sitting ducks," one professor worried. "They can pick us up at any time."

LOST PURCHASING POWER

By forbidding Sudanese citizens to own foreign currencies, the new government made international trade difficult. Wealthy Sudanese left the country or invested their money outside of Sudan. Both industrial and agricultural production slowed. Adding to the problem, some Western countries stopped providing Sudan with development assistance because Bashir had overthrown a democratically elected government.

The cost of war drove the government further into debt. The Sudanese pound dropped in value, and prices kept rising. By the mid-1990s, Sudan was the world's largest debtor to the World Bank and the International Monetary Fund. The Sudanese people were far worse off economically than they had been before the coup.

Bashir's answer to inflation was to force vendors to sell goods at lower prices. But as prices were slashed, goods simply disappeared from stores. Instead, an underground economy flourished, driving prices up even higher.

Ten years later, with the end of the civil war and growing oil production, Sudan's economy began to improve. Successful new agribusinesses exported wheat, sorghum, peanuts, and tomatoes. But the economic rebound did not help everyone. Even as Sudanese ships carried Sudanese produce to Arab countries across the Red Sea, starving people in war-torn Darfur depended on international aid groups for food.

A SUDANESE MAN CARRIES A SACK OF GRAIN THAT WAS AIR DROPPED
into the country by the UN's World Food Programme in the late 1990s.

REFUGEES AND IDPS

The greatest changes for the greatest number of people during the Bashir regime have been the result of war. War was already part of everyday life in part of Sudan before the coup, but its resumption in 1989 and the constant hostilities since then in southern and eastern Sudan, the Nuba Mountains, and Darfur uprooted millions of Sudanese and left them without homes, livelihoods, and communities.

About half a million Sudanese have fled to neighboring countries or beyond. Many have started new lives outside Sudan, not knowing when or if they can ever go back. Many others do not have the means to begin again elsewhere and wait in refugee camps near the Sudanese borders of Chad, Ethiopia, or Kenya, hoping that

THESE SUDANESE REFUGEES HAVE TAKEN SHELTER AT A CAMP IN CHAD.

Refugees live in camps, waiting for the war in Darfur to end so they can go home.

the war will end and they can return home.

Millions more are not refugees but internally displaced persons, marking time within their homeland but unable to go home. Civilian displacement often occurs in war zones. The Sudanese army and its militias, however, have engaged in a wholesale uprooting of people and a scorched earth destruction of homes, villages, and fields. These relocations of certain ethnic groups to IDP camps in Sudan reflected government policy.

Ownership of the oil fields was an important reason for the government to remove all Nuer and Dinka people along the north-south border during the 1990s. The government so thoroughly cleared all evidence of their villages and farms that on his first visit to the area, the head of the Canadian oil company Talisman remarked, "It's obvious there has never been anyone here."[49] Similar tactics destroyed communities near the railway line that linked the north to the south. Nuba and Ingessana people in Southern Kordofan and eastern Sudan were forcibly relocated to so-called peace villages so that their land could be sold to agribusinesses and developed into large mechanized farms.

"People find free services in the [IDP] camps . . . free medical care, free water, [and] free electricity. . . . Some of these people have rented out their houses in the city and left off for the camps."

—Omar al-Bashir, interview on al-Jazeera television (an Arabic news network), March 29, 2006

By grouping displaced people in camps, the government also gained better control of their activities. Camps located near agricultural or industrial developments financed by the government or wealthy Nile Valley businessmen provided cheap labor. The camps also made the people dependent on the government and easier to control.

Since the Comprehensive Peace Agreement in 2005, an estimated one million southern Sudanese have left IDP camps to return to their homes in the south or to settle elsewhere. Some return on their own, while others wait for help from the government or the UN. Official repatriation programs are often delayed. In November 2007, the Internal Displacement Monitoring Center of the Norwegian Refugee Council calculated that six million Sudanese were still internally displaced, making Sudan's the largest internally displaced population in the world.

Not all displaced Sudanese are in camps. An undetermined number—

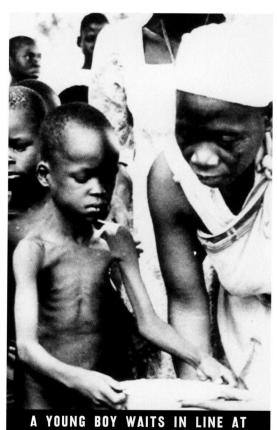

A YOUNG BOY WAITS IN LINE AT a Sudanese IDP camp for a bowl of food. Shortages of food and water are a problem at camps.

perhaps more than one million—are scattered elsewhere. Some get by on odd jobs, theft, or begging in shantytowns near large cities. Others forage for wild foods in the countryside.

Those within the camps often face inadequate housing, poor sanitary facilities, food and water shortages, exposure to outbreaks of disease, and hostile attacks from government forces suspicious of rebel activity. In 2009 the numbers of IDPs in Darfur were still rising.

SLAVERY

In the upheavals of the scorched-earth warfare the Bashir government practiced, many women and children were captured and sold into slavery. Village raids supplied many of the captives. The military supply trains to Wau in southern Sudan became infamous for the large numbers of women and children that soldiers and PDF forces guarding the train seized as "war booty" along the way.

These captives often became unpaid household servants. On call at all hours of the day and night, many slept on kitchen floors or in sheds and survived on whatever the family threw away. Their masters and mistresses could be very cruel, sometimes insulting, beating, and sexually abusing them. One woman branded the young girl who was her slave with a hot pan, saying it was "in case she got lost."

Slavery was not just a source of free labor. It was also part of the government's policy of converting non-Muslim Sudanese to Islam and Arabic culture. While serving in the homes of well-to-do northerners, southern houseboys learned Arabic and Islamic religion and customs. Southern women slaves were often forced to become wives or concubines of male owners and to bear their children. This, too, was seen as a way of spreading Arab culture, as the children would be considered Arab.

Some northern Sudanese saw nothing wrong with the practice. They believed they were doing captive southerners a favor by taking them away from war-torn areas, giving them homes, and educating them. Much of the international community responded with horror. People in many Western nations donated money to buy the freedom of these people. The publicity helped reduce the practice, although it has not entirely disappeared.

"Army officers, when they return from the South, often bring black children with them. They hand them out to relatives, for work around the house. People don't see it as slavery. But that's what it is. President Bashir himself has two or three children he found in the south. And of course the children are raised as Muslims. It's part of the government's campaign to Arabize the country."
—Ushari Mahmud, Sudanese researcher on modern-day slavery in Sudan, in an interview with a U.S. journalist, January 1999

MABIOR'S STORY

Among the stories human rights workers have collected from enslaved children who managed to escape their captors is that of Mabior (not his real name).

One morning in 1992, army soldiers surrounded Mabior's village school in southern Sudan and loaded all the children on trucks. An officer took Mabior and another eight-year-old Dinka boy from the group. He gave them Arab names and put them to work doing all the housework in his mother's home. They mopped, dusted, washed dishes and clothes, and went to market. The boys slept in one bed and ate leftovers. When the master was dissatisfied with their work, he beat and insulted them, calling Dinka people "bad" and "primitive." He also sexually abused both of the boys.

After two years, the boys confided their problems to a Dinka man they met in the marketplace, and he tried to help them legally. But the master and his family intimidated the boys, making them afraid to testify against them. Concerned people finally kidnapped the children and gave them their freedom. When a human rights worker interviewed Mabior in 1995, he had still not found his mother and his brothers, whom he had not seen in three years.

CHILD SOLDIERS

When Bashir's efforts at recruiting PDF troops fell far short of his intentions, the government turned to drafting children. Boys as young as twelve were hauled off public buses and rounded up at sports fields and recreation centers. Without notifying their parents, army recruiters trucked them immediately to army bases for training. When anxious parents mobbed army recruiting tents searching for their sons, stone-faced soldiers claimed no knowledge of their children.

Security forces also rounded up street children in cities and placed them in camps in the countryside, often near army bases. Not all the children taken to the camps were homeless orphans, as the government claimed. Children who happened to be running errands for their families or were outside playing with friends were carried off as well. Their parents did not know what became of their children—they simply disappeared. Finding their children and getting legal help to get them back often took years. These children provided another source of young soldiers. Their service was said to be voluntary, but some boys signed up for the army in order to get away from the camps. They hoped that the army would be easier to escape from than the isolated and closely guarded camps. In some cases, it was.

Most of the underage soldiers drafted into the army and the militias came from army raids in the south and other war zones. One Dinka boy was only ten when he was captured and forced to serve in the army in 1991. He managed to escape four years later. During raids in the Nuba Mountains, Sudanese forces seized six hundred Nuba boys between the ages of nine and fourteen and sent them to military bases for religious instruction and war training.

The army also abducted boys living in southern towns held by government forces. In January 1995, army recruiters found fourteen teenage boys swimming in the Nile after school. The recruiters only allowed them to get dressed, and then took them to the airport and flew them to a boot camp in eastern Sudan. Together with other new recruits, they underwent military training and Islamic indoctrination. Their instructors told them they would be fighting in a holy war and, if they died, they would only reach Paradise if they converted to Islam.

In recruiting children, the Sudanese army was doing exactly what it criticized the SPLA for doing. Southern forces also depended on underage soldiers trained together in special camps. When government troops captured SPLA child soldiers, they used the boys for propaganda purposes, giving them prominent press coverage. The government announced that the boys would receive a free education. Instead, the boys were beaten and pressured to convert to Islam.

THESE CHILD SOLDIERS WITH THE SUDANESE PEOPLE'S LIBERATION ARMY (SPLA) wait for their commander in 2001. Young boys have been forced to become soldiers in both northern and southern Sudan.

THE LOST BOYS OF SUDAN

So many children fled from war zones, particularly in southern Sudan, to avoid being recruited or enslaved that "Lost Boys of Sudan" has become a well-known phrase all around the world. The label is also a badge of honor to those who survived the ordeal. Banding together to help one another out, the boys trekked through jungles and swamps, hoping to find refuge in Ethiopia or Kenya. Many died along the way, victims of drownings, snakebites, wild animal attacks, or starvation. Some walked for years, their routes circling around enemy-held territories. Others were captured and

THESE LOST BOYS OF SUDAN HUDDLE TOGETHER AT A REFUGEE CAMP IN Kenya in 1992.

escaped again. Thousands reached refugee camps. Some were later reunited with their families, while others grew up orphans in the crowded camps with other lost children as their only family.

Not all the Lost Boys of Sudan were boys. A few girls also fled and were among the twenty-seven thousand Sudanese children who made it to refugee camps. Fewer than one hundred girls were among the thirty-eight hundred Sudanese children from refugee camps that the International Rescue Committee brought to the United States in 2001. That is because most captured girls were made personal slaves and watched closely. Boys, on the other hand, were often taken in large groups to work camps, where it was easier to find a means of escape. Also, many boys herded cattle and were not at home at the time their village was attacked. They ran away after discovering their homes destroyed and their families dead or missing.

Lopez Lomong was only six in 1991 when a government-backed militia captured him while he attended Catholic Mass in a village in southern Sudan. Older boys who knew his family helped him escape, and they walked for days to reach a refugee camp in Kenya. Lomong spent ten years growing up in the camp with other Lost Boys of Sudan before being resettled in the United States. He thought he was an orphan, but in 2003, he learned that his mother was still alive and looking for him in Kenya.

Now a U.S. citizen and a champion runner, Lomong won a place on the U.S. Olympic track team in 2008 and was selected to carry the U.S. flag at the opening ceremonies in Beijing, China. "Before, I ran from danger and death. Now I run for sport," he said, adding that it is "an honor to represent the country that saved me and showed me the way."

CHAPTER 5

CENSORSHIP

BASHIR'S PLANS FOR AN ISLAMIST REPUBLIC IN SUDAN called for a massive indoctrination of the Sudanese people. Many Muslims disagreed with these Islamist views. Although about 70 percent of Sudanese are Muslim, Islamic fundamentalist parties had never won the support of more than a quarter of Sudanese voters. First, Bashir had to silence the voices of everyone opposed to the National Islamic Front's agenda. Then he could have free rein to conquer the minds of all Sudanese through the spread of Islamist propaganda.

The night of the June 30, 1989, coup, army troops occupied radio and television stations. Military music replaced regular programming. As the regime got under way, Bashir put NIF activists and sympathizers in control of radio and television programming. But the coup came at a time when electronic communications were expanding. Sudanese with shortwave radios could reach the British

PROPAGANDA

ACCESS TO THE INTERNET IS ONE WAY THAT SOME SUDANESE PEOPLE received information from sources other than the government. These Sudanese surf the Internet at a café in Khartoum.

Broadcasting Corporation (BBC), Voice of America, and other distant stations. Satellite dishes brought CNN, BBC-TV, al-Jazeera, and other Arab and international programming to middle-class Sudanese. Few listened to or watched the government's propaganda. During the 1990s, the Internet began to supply more sources of information.

PRESS CENSORSHIP

Bashir was more successful at censoring the press. The night of the coup, soldiers also barged into Sudan's many newspaper offices, stopping presses and seizing all copies that were already printed. Only the *Armed Forces*, a daily newspaper, was allowed to publish.

The military government later sponsored two newspapers, mainly staffed by NIF loyalists. To keep up the appearance of being nonpolitical, the government permitted a few non-NIF journalists to work for these periodicals. Since the newspaper shutdowns had left about twelve thousand journalists unemployed, the authorities assumed these reporters would be grateful for the work and not cause trouble. Besides, government censors vetted every article before publication.

The foreign press in Sudan was also required to submit to censorship of its reports. The government controlled the number of foreign reporters in Sudan by revoking visas or not granting them. Journalists who did not comply with government regulations, even those who were NIF party members, faced harassment by the police or arrest.

In 1993 Bashir issued the Press and Publications Act, which set up an agency to monitor newspapers and magazines. The first independent newspaper since the coup appeared in early 1994. Within a few weeks, however, security forces raided its offices and arrested the editor, a leading NIF member, for printing an article the censors had not approved. By April it was shut down entirely. It was banned, the government explained, "for raising doubts about the purpose and struggle of the armed forces and People's [Popular] Defense Forces" with the aim of "destroying the revolution."

INTERNET BLOGS

The Internet has given opponents of the Bashir regime the freedom of expression the media does not have within Sudan. Newspaper editors who find their articles withdrawn by the censors sometimes e-mail them to subscribers. They may also post them on a sympathetic website or blog, so long as they are able to do so anonymously.

Many anti-Bashir blogs, in Arabic, English, and other languages, appear on the Internet. These blogs are posted by Sudanese exiles safely beyond the reach of Bashir's security forces. These blogs keep alive resistance to Bashir and supply the Sudanese people with uncensored information and opinions. Only about 9 percent of the people living in Sudan, however, own computers, and either technological problems or government controls occasionally block some sites.

More local newspapers appeared before the elections in 1996, but none survived past July. Yet journalists fought back. In spite of repeated harassment that included suspension, arrests, stiff fines, beatings, and banning. More newspapers—most in Arabic and a few in English—kept sprouting up. The independent press occasionally managed to slip articles past the censors with information on the fighting in the south and on government corruption. Sometimes editors simply left blank spaces where censored articles were supposed to have appeared, a practice the government forbade.

Since 2003 Bashir has repeatedly promised to end press censorship. The Interim National Constitution, approved in 2005, guarantees freedom of expression and press freedom. Crackdowns still occur against independent newspapers, however, and journalists who criticize the government are still arrested or called in for questioning. The government also tries to keep journalists from reporting on sensitive issues by restricting their travel. In 2009 the independent press in Sudan was still working in a climate of fear.

SUPPRESSING CULTURE

Another target of censorship during Bashir's regime has been popular music, dancing, and traditional celebrations considered un-Islamic by NIF leaders. Popular songs quickly disappeared from the airwaves after the coup. The Khartoum Public Order Act later denounced as "trivial" all "songs that use words or expressions contradicting religion, morality, good taste, and good conscience." The act banned all concerts and broadcasts of such music.

Radio stations erased tapes of popular singers or simply taped over the songs with sermons and Islamist propaganda. Not all music was banished. Songs praising jihad (Islamic holy war) and the Popular Defense Forces frequently aired. Occasionally Sudanese folk music or Western music made the cut, so long as it contained no mention of wine, kisses, women's bodies, or politics.

Among the singers not suppressed are *hakkama* singers, women whose songs encourage the janjawiid militias to kill, rape, and loot as they attack non-Arab villages. "The blood of the blacks runs like water," says one hakkama song. "We take their goods and we chase them from our area and our cattle will be in their land!" Local authorities in Darfur have rewarded women with cash, gold, and jewelry for composing and singing these lyrics.

Other musicians faced harassment. They might be arrested, questioned, beaten, and their instruments smashed. Before being released, they were often forced to write and sign assurances that they would not perform objectionable songs—ones that mentioned poverty, famine, or anything else that suggested political protest.

Dancing was also suppressed. The Morality Monitoring Unit of the General Administration of Public Order targeted weddings and other celebrations where the forbidden "dancing between men and women" might take place. It also closed down nightclubs and confiscated mobile discos that once thrived in poor neighborhoods of Khartoum.

Security police broke up traditional ceremonies, such as Zar dancing as well. The Zar is a form of ritual dancing to drums that is practiced mainly by women as a way to relieve stress, a kind of dance psychotherapy. It may also involve a sacrificed animal, which the dancers share as a meal at the conclusion of the ceremony. Although the Bashir regime officially banned Zar dancing in 1992, it remains popular in spite of police raids, arrests, and confiscation of drums.

ZAR MUSICIANS PERFORM THEIR healing ritual in Egypt. Zar dancing has been banned in Sudan, but people still secretly participate in the ceremonies.

RELIGIOUS PERSECUTION

The Bashir regime also took steps to suppress or discourage all non-Islamist religious activity. Without officially banning Christianity, Judaism, or other religions, the government made non-Muslims second-class citizens. Non-Muslims who supervised Muslims in government offices lost their jobs. Sudanese who practiced traditional African religions were the most openly discriminated against.

> *"We are at the other end of the bullet. We are the target of Islamic belligerence, the object of this holy war."*
>
> —Catholic leader in Sudan, 1992

Government officials disrupted the humanitarian work of charities supported by other religions. They denied permits for the construction of churches. They also took over Christian schools and ordered the destruction of some churches and Christian schools under the pretext of slum clearance.

Christian clergy found it difficult to obtain travel permits. During peace talks between the government and the SPLA in Nairobi, the government prevented the archbishop of Khartoum from attending. Security forces also detained clergy for alleged offenses.

Some of the harshest measures affected Muslims. Any Muslim who left Islam for another religion could be accused of apostasy (abandoning a religious faith), which carried the death sentence. The Bashir regime also seized the property of mosques belonging to sects associated with opposition parties. The most important of these was the shrine with the tomb of the Mahdi, which the government confiscated in 1993. The government forced worshippers to accept government-appointed imams (Muslim clergy). Religious leaders whose Friday sermons criticized the government—among them Sadiq al-Mahdi—were arrested.

EDUCATION

STUDENTS AT SUDAN UNIVERSITY attend class in 1993. The educational system underwent many changes after Bashir took control.

To convert all Sudanese to his Islamist views, Bashir started with the schools. He had employees of the ministry of education who were not members of NIF dismissed and replaced with NIF activists. At the universities, Bashir replaced administrators with NIF sympathizers and abolished elected faculty unions. Then he doubled the number of students at the established universities and added nine

BLOCKING CROSS-CULTURAL EXCHANGE

Efforts by the Bashir regime to isolate Sudan from Western influences included closing down PLAN, an international charity that encouraged children to send pictures and letters to one another to promote cross-cultural understanding. In 1992 the Sudanese government accused PLAN of using the program to undermine Islam and banned all direct communication between Sudanese and Western children. The charity, which has no religious, political, or governmental ties, considers direct communication an important aspect of its work and decided to cease operations in Sudan. When PLAN withdrew, about twenty thousand Sudanese children lost pen pals in donor countries. Their families and villages also lost the twenty-two dollars contributed every month to PLAN by sponsors of the children.

new universities in provincial capitals around the country.

The curriculum quickly changed. Arabic became the language of instruction in all public schools and universities, and all students, regardless of their religion, were required to study Islam.

The government also took over private and foreign schools, including those run by Christian missionaries. Only two, the Khartoum American School and the British Unity High School, also in Khartoum, were allowed to remain independent. Their students, however, were not permitted to take the entrance exams for Sudanese universities.

PROPAGANDA CAMPS

Bashir's educational program included street children in the cities, who were taken to special camps. A few camps were in Khartoum, but most were in isolated areas far from town to prevent escape. The largest one, located two hours' drive north of Khartoum, held as many as one thousand boys. They lived in thatch-roofed huts with eight or ten beds to a room. Girls went to a separate camp. The camps had schools where the children learned Arabic and Islam, as well as practical skills such as metalworking (for the boys) and embroidery (for the girls).

Although many of the children were Dinka or Nuba and practiced traditional religions or Christianity, all had to take part in Islamic prayers. Children who sang hymns or performed any religious ritual that was not Islamic were flogged. Teachers also gave children with non-Arab names, such as Deng or Akol, new Arab names, such as Ahmed, Ali, or Muhammad.

Bashir spread Islamist propaganda to adults through the Popular Defense Forces. He required all civil servants, teachers, professors, and university students to undergo three months of PDF training. The number of people attending PDF camps increased in 1994, when every male between the ages of eighteen and thirty could be drafted to serve in the army. Besides basic military training, these camps provided a rigorous schedule of religious instruction. It began with dawn prayers and lasted late into the night. Bashir described the training as a "school for national and spiritual education" through which "the Sudanese citizen's mind can be remolded and his religious consciousness enhanced" in order to help the regime "restructure and purify society."

MEMBERS OF THE SUDANESE POPULAR DEFENSE FORCES ATTEND military training camp in 1998. The camps also trained adults in religious studies.

Peace villages aimed to convert non-Muslim and non-Arabic-speaking ethnic groups to Islamist views. By moving whole populations, such as the Nuba of Southern Kordofan and the Ingessana of Blue Nile State, away from their homelands, the government hoped to stamp out indigenous customs and beliefs. Children, who made up 80 percent of the population of these villages, attended schools where they learned Arabic and Islamic religion by reading the Quran. Women also received religious and language instruction, and the few men in the villages were forcibly circumcised. Circumcision, the ritual removal of some or all of the foreskin of the penis, is not usually customary among non-Muslim Africans.

In June 1998, the government celebrated the success of its Islamization program with a mass ceremony for sixteen hundred men and women from southern Sudan and the Nuba Mountains who had converted to Islam. A government official pressured them to be the "vanguard [forefront] for Islam" in southern Sudan and help to spread Islam across the nation.

CHAPTER 6
MAINTAINING

BASHIR WAS A LITTLE-KNOWN OFFICER IN THE SUDANESE ARMY
when he gained international attention as the leader of a military junta
in 1989. Few people expected that he would remain in power for long.
But Bashir has led the country for longer than any other Sudanese
head of government since Sudan became independent in 1956.
Various maneuvers have contributed to the longevity of his regime.

In a tactic used by many other dictators, Bashir merged the
executive and legislative branches of government into one office
to give himself the final word on all major issues. He could also
declare a state of emergency—a time when usual laws do not apply
during an emergency—to centralize control under his command.

Bashir used a two-pronged strategy to take over the judicial
branch of government too. Using the powers allowed under a state
of emergency, he set up military courts to try civilians accused

A GRIP ON POWER

BASHIR HAS HELD ONTO POWER in Sudan for many years by controlling all branches of government. Here he speaks at a rally in 1997.

in cases that he claimed concerned national security. That meant that a military tribunal could sentence any civilian protesting against the government, even peacefully. These courts not only imposed harsh punishments but also gave defendants no chance to appeal their convictions.

Bashir made significant changes to the civilian courts as well. In the first two years of his regime, he fired 128 judges

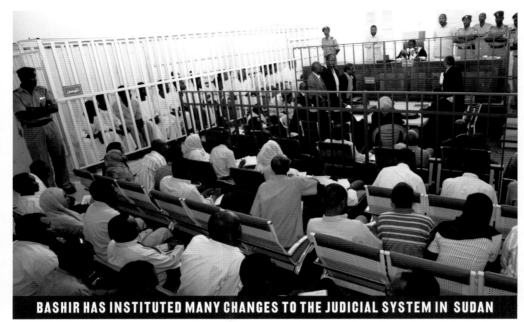

BASHIR HAS INSTITUTED MANY CHANGES TO THE JUDICIAL SYSTEM IN SUDAN since coming to power. In this courtroom in 2008, twelve alleged Darfur rebels *(behind bars at left)* were condemned to death for an attack on Khartoum.

and legal advisers to the government, among them 14 Supreme Court judges and 12 Court of Appeals judges. Then he gave himself the power to choose and appoint the chief justice of the Supreme Court. In this way, he successfully brought the judiciary under his control.

CENTRALIZING AUTHORITY

In 1991 Bashir created what he called a federal system of government, which was supposed to give each province more control over its own affairs. But laws enacted by the central government could override any laws passed by provincial assemblies. In addition, Bashir appointed all the provincial governors and administrators, and they controlled finances and education in each province.

In 1993 a new division of the country carved the nine provinces into twenty-six states. Bashir claimed that this change would bring the government closer to the people. But it also increased his control, since the central government still appointed the governors and the administrators in each state and determined their budgets.

The constitution of 1998 modified the role of the central government only slightly. Instead of appointing state governors, Bashir had the right to select three candidates for that office. The people living in each state then voted on the candidates the government had chosen.

SECURITY FORCES

Crucial to enforcing Bashir's government are his security forces. These consist of various police and army units, some of them working undercover. These agencies keep Bashir in office.

Some of these forces started as part of the NIF political party. The Guardians of Morality and Advocates of Good enforced the social laws. The People's Police were civilian committees formed as part of a Civil Defense Act in 1991. Their alleged purpose was to help out in cases of natural disasters or foreign attack. Their principal role, however, was to spy on their neighbors and report suspicious activities or infractions of the social laws, such as private parties held without permits from the authorities. They had their own firearms, courts, and places of detention, although they generally punished offenders on the spot, usually by flogging. More recently, People's Police have proved useful as volunteer informers. They infiltrate political parties and refugee camps to get information for the government.

The most dreaded of the security units was the Revolutionary Security Force, established in 1989 to oversee all security. Revolutionary Security Guards were the ones who detained and tortured political dissidents in unofficial prisons known as ghost houses.

Other security forces provide military intelligence, oversee police operations, and protect members of the government. One security force monitors Sudanese exiles. Little precise information is known about these agencies and their operations. The Revolutionary Security Force, for example, no longer exists under that name, but it may have been replaced by another secret agency. Some security forces are suspected of conveying orders and military supplies to the janjawiid militias in Darfur. A high-level army officer told Human Rights Watch in 2005, "Security controls this country."

ELIMINATING RIVALS

Bashir's greatest fear from the beginning was the possibility of another military coup. Soon after seizing power, he fired all army officers not sympathetic to NIF policies, especially commanders with ranks higher than his own. By 1993 about 1,500 officers had been let go. This policy continued even though the regime needed good military leadership for the war it was fighting in southern Sudan. In 1995 Bashir fired 227 more officers, including 57 brigadiers and other generals.

Bashir also dismissed members of his Revolutionary Command Council who disagreed with his policies. Two dismissed members had been key conspirators in the coup, but they opposed the execution of twenty-eight army officers in April 1990. A Nuba member of the RCC who had been head of national security was demoted to minister of youth and sports when Nuba leaders asked Bashir for official investigations into Nuba deaths and disappearances.

Frequent shifts in cabinet posts kept loyal supporters close and moved out less trusted appointees. These changes in Bashir's cabinet also increased NIF control. By 1995 Islamists led every aspect of government.

In 1999, when Hassan al-Turabi attempted to oust Bashir from office, Bashir quickly struck back. He used state of emergency power to quash Turabi's attempts to impeach him. The emergency

HASSAN AL-TURABI *(LEFT)* TRIED TO UNSUCCESSFULLY OUST OMAR AL-Bashir *(right)* from the presidency in 1999.

allowed him to suspend parliament and arrest his former mentor and ally. Turabi, however, remains a potent enemy with a large following among Islamists in Sudan. A close associate of Turabi heads the Justice and Equality Movement in Darfur. This Islamist group has played a major role in the Darfur rebellion and may, with international help, succeed in bringing down Bashir.

FAKE DEMOCRACY

Essential to remaining in power was Bashir's plan to make the NIF regime's dictatorship look like a legitimate government chosen by the Sudanese. This was important because the government needed loyal citizens to help carry out its agenda of uniting the country into an Islamist state. It was also necessary to gain legitimacy in the eyes of the world. Sudan wanted to maintain its memberships in various international organizations, such as the Organization of African Unity, the United Nations, and the Arab League. Sudan needed to be able to negotiate with neighboring countries on numerous issues. It also wanted to develop trade relations and receive development aid from the International Monetary Fund, the World Bank, and donor nations. For these reasons, the regime set about creating a government that appeared democratic. At the same time, to stay in power, it was just as important to prevent real democracy.

When the Transitional National Assembly, appointed by the NIF regime, began to meet in 1992, most of its members were NIF leaders or sympathizers. But leaders of major ethnic groups were also given seats to make the body look more democratic. The

BASHIR IS ESCORTED BY A UNITED NATIONS OFFICIAL AS HE WALKS TO the podium to deliver a speech at a UN aid conference in 2008. Maintaining relationships with organizations such as the UN is very important to Bashir.

government also hoped that giving them a role would help gain their support.

The plan backfired in the case of Aldo Ajo Deng, a Dinka who served as deputy speaker in the assembly. In December 1993, Deng denounced the government for human rights violations and fled to London. Deng was not the only assembly member to criticize the government. But since the assembly had no real power, the regime simply ignored any recommendations for change.

In 1993, when Bashir dissolved the RCC and took the title of president, his purpose was again to make his regime seem more legitimate. Elections were part of this charade. When they were finally held in March 1996, no political parties and only twelve days of campaigning were allowed. No major Sudanese politicians bothered to oppose Bashir in what was clearly going to be a rigged election. Bashir won 75.7 percent of the votes cast.

Parliamentary elections were also held in 1996. Almost one-third of the members were elected ahead of the general election at a NIF convention. Elections were canceled in the southern states for so-called security reasons, and 50 of the remaining 275 seats were filled by NIF party members who ran unopposed. This was when longtime NIF leader Hassan al-Turabi became speaker of the new assembly.

In 1998 Bashir presented a constitution to the Sudanese. The people allegedly approved it in a referendum, but Bashir's opponents challenged the vote as rigged. The new constitution guaranteed a broad range of human rights, but it still allowed Bashir to suspend many of those rights on the "occurrence or approach of any emergent danger."

BASHIR CELEBRATES HIS 1996 presidential election by holding a staff, a Sudanese symbol of power.

The vague wording assured that Bashir and his security forces could still silence opponents. The provision later gave Bashir the legal means to defeat Turabi's attempt to oust him from the presidency.

Elections in 2000 reestablished Bashir's control over Sudan. He has remained in office since then because the Comprehensive Peace Agreement signed in 2005 postponed elections for another four years. Various groups have urged further postponement.

> "No one's interested in these elections. Who would they vote for? All the candidates are government candidates."
>
> —Tayyeb al-Abbasi, an official of the Democratic Unionist Party, during elections in Sudan, December 2000

The Interim National Constitution that replaces the constitution of 1998 is largely based on that document. The presidency still controls the judiciary, security forces, and the commissions on human rights and elections. It does, however, include a bill of rights and allows states to elect their own governors. Most important, the national legislature will have to approve declared states of emergency.

CHAPTER 7

MAKING FRIENDS

SADIQ AL-MAHDI'S CHAOTIC ADMINISTRATION from 1986 to 1989 had dismayed many of Sudan's neighbors and trading partners. After the coup, they hoped Bashir's military junta would bring more peace and stability to the country. "Given the failure of the civilian government," the British newspaper the *Times* declared, "the arrival of the military government promising an end to war can be welcomed. When Sudan has peace, it shall be able to decide whether its long term interests are best served by a military rule."

Egypt, Sudan's northern neighbor, was the first country to establish diplomatic relations with the Revolutionary Command Council. Saudi Arabia recognized the RCC soon after, saying Saudi Arabia considered the regime change an "internal affair" and hoped to continue "its brotherly economic and political ties with Sudan." Iraq and other Arab countries followed suit.

AND

ENEMIES

The United States stopped economic and military aid to Sudan at the time of the coup. That was because a law Congress passed in 1986 requires that all nonhumanitarian aid cease if a military junta overthrows a democratically elected government in any country. But the United States remained optimistic that Bashir would restore democracy to Sudan, and President George H. W. Bush made plans to ask Congress to waive the law. Congress did not stop funding for projects that were already approved.

Bashir's earliest diplomatic overtures sought allies for his regime in other Islamist and Arab nations. His first journey abroad as head of government was to Iran, but because Bashir had not yet revealed his Islamist goals to the Sudanese, he kept this journey secret. The following year, as the regime's ties to NIF became public, Iran began sending members of its Revolutionary Guards to help Sudanese military officers train Sudan's Popular Defense Forces and People's Police. Iran's Revolutionary Guards are special military forces trained in security operations, police enforcement, and missle warfare.

Bashir also visited Libyan leader Muammar al-Qaddafi in Tripoli, the capital of Libya. Qaddafi had his own ideas about uniting Arabs and welcomed Bashir. Qaddafi was ready to supply oil, weapons, and tactical support for the Sudanese army. In July 1989, the two leaders signed a Union Treaty calling for a merger of Sudan and Libya. Bashir later praised the treaty as "a first step towards the full unity of the Arab world."

When Sudan's war in the south resumed, Libyan pilots flew bombing missions against the SPLA. In return, Bashir allowed Libyan troops to use western Sudan as a base to attack Chad. At the time, Chad was involved in a civil war similar to Sudan's. In Chad, however, the Christian and animist southerners held power and northern Muslims were the rebels. Qaddafi wanted to overthrow the president of Chad, southerner Hissène Habré, and replace him with a Muslim from northern Chad. In December 1990, the Chadian rebels, with Libyan help, defeated Habré and made Idriss Déby president of Chad.

BECOMING A PARIAH STATE

As Bashir's Islamist agenda became clearer, the good relations that Bashir had initiated with Arab countries began turning sour. President Hosni Mubarak of Egypt was especially wary of having an Islamist regime as a neighbor. For decades Egyptian leaders had been fearful that Islamic fundamentalists would try to overthrow them by violent means. Egypt was the birthplace of the Muslim Brotherhood, a militant Islamist organization with branches in many countries. It spread to Sudan in the 1940s, where its members formed the political parties Islamic Charter Front and later the NIF. Mubarak quickly granted Bashir's political opponents asylum in Egypt. Leaders of Sudan's outlawed political parties gathered in Cairo, the Egyptian capital, to carry on the work of the National Democratic Alliance, an organization first formed by political prisoners in Khartoum's Kobar Prison in October 1989. These party leaders met to plan ways to defeat the Bashir regime.

Bashir lost more support in August 1990, when Iraq invaded and annexed Kuwait, its small, oil-rich neighbor. The Islamic Conference Organization, a group of forty-five countries at that time, stretching from western Africa to Indonesia, called on Iraq to withdraw from Kuwait. Sudan was the only member to abstain from voting on the issue. Bashir continued to support President Saddam Hussein of Iraq right through the Persian Gulf War in January and February 1991. Egypt, Saudi Arabia, and other states around the Persian Gulf withdrew their economic aid to Sudan and sent home thousands of Sudanese who had been working in their countries.

Bashir's support for Saddam Hussein tipped the scales for other donor nations as well. The United States and the European Union were already growing alarmed at Bashir's actions. For Western nations, his friendships with Iran and Libya, his Islamist policies, his disregard for human rights, and his resumption of the civil war were all red flags. After Bashir sided with Saddam Hussein, the United States put aside all thoughts of resuming aid, although it did not break off diplomatic relations. It was important to keep a dialogue going between the two nations, to protect U.S. interests in Sudan (such as the Chevron Corporation's oil business) and to monitor humanitarian aid in the war-torn south. The European Union, the world's leading donor of aid, also cut off economic and military donations to Sudan in 1990. The loss to Bashir was sizable. Both the United States and the EU had been funding many development projects, as well as such "nonlethal" military assistance as repairing aircraft and trucks and supplying communications equipment and spare parts.

Meanwhile, Bashir's Islamist policies made Sudan a magnet for persecuted Islamists. In March 1990, Bashir declared an open door for all "Arab brothers"—no Arab would need a visa to enter Sudan. Members of the Muslim Brotherhood and other national and international Islamist groups from Egypt, Eritrea, Algeria, Tunisia, and Uganda flocked to Sudan to escape harassment or arrest in their own countries. Among the refugees was Osama bin Laden, the son of a wealthy Saudi Arabian businessman with close connections to the Saudi royal family. In 1991 bin Laden fled Saudi Arabia, where he had been under house arrest for denouncing his government's role in the Persian Gulf War. Hassan al-Turabi invited him to Sudan. Other dissident groups, some notorious for political violence in Syria, Lebanon, and Libya, also found a safe haven in Sudan. Rumors circulated of terrorist training camps for Muslim radicals preparing to export Islamic revolution.

In 1993 the United States put Sudan on its list of state sponsors of terrorism. This list, started in 1979, identifies countries that the U.S. secretary of state has determined to have repeatedly supported acts of international terrorism by giving safe haven and material assistance to terrorist organizations. By 1993 the whole world was aware of Sudan's links to terrorism. In February terrorists had driven a rental truck full of explosives into the garage of the World Trade Center in New York City and detonated a bomb that killed five people and injured more than one thousand. Five of

FIREFIGHTERS AND OTHER RESCUE workers respond to the terrorist bombing at the World Trade Center in New York City in 1993.

the fifteen men indicted in connection with the bombing were Sudanese citizens. Sheikh Omar Abdel Rahman, an Egyptian cleric accused of sanctioning the bombing, had acquired his visa to the United States in Khartoum. And some of the suspects in the conspiracy had extensive contact with two Sudanese diplomats at UN headquarters in New York City before the bombings. Sudan was rapidly becoming a "pariah state"—a country that shows so little respect for international standards of behavior that few nations want to have diplomatic or commercial relations with it.

POROUS BORDERS

Sudan's neighbors could not escape the threat to their own stability. As they watched Sudan help Libya bring about a regime change in Chad, other leaders worried about the security of their own positions—and with reason. With largely unguarded borders in a landscape with few roads, it was not easy to control movements from one country to the other.

In 1994 Eritrea broke off relations with Sudan for giving asylum and aid to the Eritrean Islamic Jihad. This group was plotting to overthrow the government of the newly independent nation. In reprisal, Eritrea welcomed exiled Sudanese politicians and sponsored conferences of the exiles' group, the National Democratic Alliance, in its capital, Asmara.

The following year, Uganda broke off relations with Sudan because Sudan supported an extremist Christian faction trying to overthrow the Ugandan government. The alliance of the Islamist Sudanese army and the Ugandan rebels who called themselves the Lord's Resistance Army (LRA) was one of the stranger results of the civil war. The LRA needed guns, and the Sudanese army needed anyone willing to fight the SPLA, which had been uniting southern factions into a cohesive force.

In 1995 Egypt issued a report with detailed information on about twenty terrorist training camps in Sudan. The report revealed that Iran's Revolutionary Guards and Afghan veterans were running the camps. Trainees came from Egypt, Eritrea, Ethiopia, Uganda, Algeria, and Tunisia. Fundamentalist groups known for using violence, such as Hamas, Hezbollah, and Islamic Jihad, were represented at the camps.

That year Sudan helped Egyptian Islamists in a plot to assassinate Egypt's president Hosni Mubarak, who was attending a meeting in Addis Ababa, Ethiopia. The attempt failed, but Sudan's complicity in the attack increased international opposition to the Bashir regime. When Sudan refused to honor a treaty with Ethiopia providing for the extradition (surrender to another country for trial) of three suspects in the case, the UN Security Council imposed sanctions on Sudan.

UN sanctions include a range of nonmilitary measures, such as restrictions on trade or travel. The resolution passed in April 1996 requested that all nations "significantly reduce the number and the level" of Sudanese diplomats posted in their countries and limit their travel within their countries. The council also asked them to refuse entry to their countries of Sudanese government officials and members of Sudanese armed forces. The resolution further instructed international and regional organizations not to hold conferences in Sudan. It was a humiliating blow to Bashir's efforts to gain international support for his regime.

FINDING FRIENDS

As Bashir's Sudan grew more isolated from the world community, Bashir looked for help from other pariah states. One was Iran. In December 1991, President Ali Akbar Hashemi Rafsanjani visited Khartoum with a delegation of 150 Iranians. He promised loans, Iranian oil, financing for Chinese weapons, and more Iranian Revolutionary Guards. Two years later, Iran reportedly financed about twenty Chinese aircraft for Sudan.

Iraq also remained a good friend to Sudan. Iraq was ready to support Bashir's regime with financial help and technical assistance from military and civilian experts. In exchange, Iraq wanted Sudan to provide a place where Iraq could produce chemical weapons away from United Nations inspectors. Sudan supplied a heavily guarded military complex where Iraqi employees could carry out their work in secret.

Sudan engaged in legitimate trade with Iraq as well. One Sudanese product sent to Iraq, a deworming medicine for cattle, was produced at a pharmaceutical plant in Khartoum. Such legal exports helped to cover the illegal traffic in banned chemicals.

China became another lifeline for Bashir. After the Chinese military violently suppressed student protests in Tiananmen Square in Beijing, China, in June 1989, the United States, the European Union, Japan, and other countries imposed numerous sanctions on trade with China. To overcome this commercial isolation, China looked to develop new markets. Paid perhaps by Iran, China began shipping fighter planes, tanks, and pieces of artillery to Sudan. They also sent technicians to teach the Sudanese how to use the equipment.

On a visit to Beijing in 1995, Bashir secured China's promise to develop Sudan's oil fields. China took part ownership of the Greater Nile Petroleum Operating Company and helped build an oil refinery near Khartoum and a pipeline to Port Sudan. Before

THE RELATIONSHIP BETWEEN SUDAN AND CHINA HAS BEEN IMPORTANT
to Bashir. Here he arrives in China for the China-Africa summit in 2006.

long China was Sudan's main customer for oil and its top supplier of military equipment.

YIELDING TO PRESSURE

In 1996 Sudan's international reputation reached a low point. In January the UN Security Council unanimously condemned Sudan for not extraditing the suspects in the attempted assassination of Mubarak. A month later, Eritrea made a ceremony of handing the keys to the Sudanese Embassy in Asmara to the leader of the National Democratic Alliance (NDA) so that the NDA could use the building as its headquarters. Eritrea also promised the NDA military support to overthrow Bashir.

The same month, the United States withdrew its embassy staff from Khartoum. The State Department did not break off diplomatic relations entirely but set up a scaled-back embassy in Nairobi, Kenya, to maintain contact with Sudanese officials. Sudanese foreign minister Ali Osman Taha angrily accused the United States of trying to isolate Sudan. Meanwhile, the United States continued to list Sudan as a state sponsor of terrorism, and the United Nations High Commission on Human Rights continued to appoint special rapporteurs to investigate violations of human rights in Sudan.

Bashir made some concessions. He tried to get rid of Sudan's reputation as a haven for terrorists by ousting some of the more controversial ones. In 1994 Sudan had deported a Venezuelan leftist revolutionary known as Carlos the Jackal to France, where he was wanted for numerous bombings. In 1996 Bashir expelled Osama bin Laden, who departed for Afghanistan with his terrorist group al-Qaeda.

The United States nevertheless continued to add to sanctions on trade with Sudan. In 1997 the United States prohibited the importation of any goods or services from Sudan. (One exception was gum arabic, an essential ingredient in soft drinks.) The imposition of sanctions put pressure on Bashir but also had disadvantages. By restricting travel between the two countries, the United States created barriers between Americans and Sudanese and discouraged academic and cultural exchanges that promote international understanding.

In 1998, when al-Qaeda terrorists bombed U.S. embassies in Nairobi, Kenya, and Dar es Salaam, Tanzania, the United States retaliated by bombing Sudan. Cruise missiles from U.S. naval vessels in the Red Sea demolished a pharmaceutical plant in Khartoum that the United States said was making chemical weapons for Iraq.

U.S. citizens, meanwhile, were becoming involved in helping southern Sudanese civilians. Schools and churches raised funds to buy the freedom of enslaved women and children, and whole communities became involved in the adoption, settlement, and education of the Lost Boys of Sudan.

THE UNITED STATES BOMBED THIS pharmaceutical plant near Khartoum in 1998, alleging it was making chemical weapons for Iraq.

Bashir gradually became more open to peace negotiations. The leaders of Eritrea, Ethiopia, Uganda, and Kenya played a patient and continuing role in bringing the Bashir government and the SPLM to sit down and talk peace. The United States, Britain, and Norway supported the effort as well. Bashir's outward show of moving toward democracy gave some hope of an end to military rule.

As a result, Sudan's relations with its neighbors improved. The UN Security Council ended its sanctions against Sudan in 2001. After the World Trade Center and Pentagon attacks in September of that year, Sudan agreed to cooperate with the United States in fighting terrorism. In 2002 the Machakos Protocol led the way to the Comprehensive Peace Agreement, which officially ended the civil war between northern and southern Sudan in 2005.

With Bashir's continued authoritarian rule and his handling of the uprising in Darfur, however, Sudan's international reputation plummeted once more. The African Union rejected Bashir's bid to lead the organization in 2006 and 2007. U.S. sanctions were not lifted, and the UN Security Council adopted new sanctions on Sudan in 2005. After the Darfur Peace Agreement was signed in 2006, numerous nations, including China, pressured Sudan into allowing UNAMID, a joint force of African Union and United Nations peacekeepers, to report Sudan's frequent violations. The UN High Commission for Human Rights still mandates a special rapporteur to monitor human rights abuses. Yet Sudan is not entirely friendless. Sudan has many trading partners in Asia (including China, Japan, India, and South Korea) and in Arab countries (including Saudi Arabia, Egypt, and United Arab Emirates). And in March 2009 several African and Arab countries as well as China and Russia spoke out against the warrant issued by the ICC for the arrest of Omar al-Bashir on charges of committing war crimes and crimes against humanity.

CONCLUSION

SUDAN'S

WHAT WILL HAPPEN TO OMAR AL-BASHIR? It is not easy to predict. A past master of political maneuvering with a strong base of support in the army, Bashir is well entrenched in the government of Sudan. He has grown rich on Sudan's oil and rewarded his supporters well. The constitution grants him extraordinary powers.

The limits the constitution places on him, such as having to hold elections, are the kind he has ignored in the past. Elections can be postponed, limited for "security reasons," or simply counted in his favor, especially since he chooses the election commission. If he is able to prevent outside observers and to intimidate Sudanese voters, he may be able to rig reelection to office. If he cannot manage that, the army may be willing to keep him in power.

But Bashir faces three very different opponents who may succeed in toppling his dictatorship. One is his old mentor and

FUTURE

press conference in Turkey in 2008.
No one knows how long he will
remain in power in Sudan.

present enemy, Hassan al-Turabi, the leader of the National Salvation Revolution and later the founder of the Popular National Congress Party. Since Turabi tried to impeach him in 1999, Bashir has sidelined and imprisoned Turabi, but he has not silenced him or won over his large following of dedicated Islamists. Bashir accuses Turabi of stirring up the rebellion in Darfur. The leader of one of the rebel factions in

Darfur, the Justice and Equality Movement, in fact is a follower of Turabi, but Turabi is too skillful a politician to admit a direct connection between his party and the rebels.

Turabi's resilience has been noted for a long time. "Turabi is a man with no limits," one politician observed back in 1993. "He is the man who is willing to go to the last meter and even beyond it. As far as political power is concerned, he is as hard as steel."

Although he is in his seventies, Turabi actively leads his party, which he claims is the most popular in Sudan. He readily admits his regret that he allied himself with the military to gain power in 1989. "Military rule ruined the country," he says. "Democracy is the only viable answer to Sudan's numerous challenges." Although it is unlikely that he would run for office against Bashir, his persistent criticism and backing of Bashir's opponents may help to bring the dictator down.

"We are facing a challenge and the referee is the Sudanese people. They should decide if we are really criminals, or if we are leaders of the people who should govern them in the future. I issue a challenge: if I get less than 50 per cent of the people's votes in Darfur, then truly I don't deserve to lead the country."

—Omar al-Bashir, interview with British television's Channel 4, October 17, 2008

BOTH HASSAN AL-TURABI *(LEFT)* **AND SALVA KIIR MAYARDIT** *(RIGHT)* **ARE POSSIBLE** contenders to topple Bashir's dictatorship. Turabi leads the Popular National Congress Party and backs Bashir's opponents. Mayardit is president of southern Sudan and a vice president of the national government. He has worked with Bashir to try to unite the country.

A second contender in the battle to overthrow Bashir is the vice president and the president of southern Sudan, Salva Kiir Mayardit. Kiir, a founding member of the SPLM, became its leader when John Garang was killed in a helicopter crash five months after the signing of the peace agreement in 2005. As vice president, Kiir has worked alongside Bashir in an effort to reunite Sudan. It has not been an easy assignment. In July 2008, when Bashir's indictment on charges of genocide was delivered to the International Criminal Court, Bashir sent Kiir to Uganda on a mission to urge President Yoweri Museveni to oppose the indictment, a position Kiir could hardly have endorsed. If Kiir does run for the presidency, as Garang had intended to do had

THE INTERIM CONSTITUTION

The Comprehensive Peace Agreement of 2005 provided for an interim constitution to guide the governance of Sudan in the period before elections. It includes guarantees of freedom of religion, freedom of the press, assembly, and association, equality for women, respect for indigenous languages and cultures, academic freedom, and free and compulsory education at the primary level. It also provides for the equitable distribution of Sudan's wealth.

Four levels of government are defined. At the national level, the president (Bashir) and two vice presidents, one from northern Sudan (appointed by Bashir) and one from southern Sudan (the leader of the SPLM), lead the Government of National Unity. The term of office is five years, with only one reelection possible. The two-chamber National Legislature is dominated by the National Congress Party (with 52 percent of the seats) and its 450 members are appointed by the presidency (Bashir, the two vice presidents, and the Council of Ministers).

At the next level, the government of southern Sudan is headed by the leader of the SPLM (who is also a vice president at the national level).

he lived, it will be a hard fight, since Bashir shows no signs of accepting defeat at the polls. Kiir lacks Garang's charisma and has several rivals in southern Sudan, but he has a strong base there. Darfur rebels have voiced their support for his candidacy, and he has become enough of a national figure that other marginalized groups will be likely to back him. In a fair race, he might even win.

The third level is state government with elected state governors and state legislatures, and the fourth level is local government.

Much of the interim constitution is based on the constitution of 1998. Bashir retains control of the judiciary, the national election commission, the human rights commission, and security services. One important difference is that the new constitution will put some limits on Bashir's use of states of emergency. Under the interim constitution, he must gain the approval of the National Legislature to declare a state of emergency. If approved, the state of emergency may suspend parts of the bill of rights but not the right to life, freedom from slavery and from torture, the right to a fair trial, or the ban on discrimination on the basis of race, sex, or religion. In addition, the state of emergency will lapse at the end of thirty days. To renew it, Bashir will again have to seek the approval of the National Legislature.

The constitution requires a census of all Sudan, to be completed by July 2007, and elections to be held in July 2009. In 2008 the census in southern Sudan was completed, but the census of northern Sudan remained incomplete, making it necessary to consider postponing the elections.

Bashir's strongest opponent may be the ICC. The ICC was established in 2002 to prosecute crimes of serious international concern, such as genocide, war crimes, and human rights violations, when the country where the crimes were committed has failed to act. The warrant for Bashir's arrest issued in March 2009 made Bashir the first acting head of state to be accused of such crimes by the ICC.

The African Union, the Arab League, and China argued that the court should postpone action because Bashir's arrest and trial would threaten peace and security in Sudan. Many Sudanese, including leaders of opposition parties such as Sadiq al-Mahdi, agreed with this view. Only Hassan al-Turabi spoke out in favor of the ICC and urged Bashir to turn himself in. This outspokenness landed him back in prison.

The government of Sudan has warned that all attempts to prosecute Bashir will backfire. Sudan is ready to "go further than what most imagine if the United Nations and the Security Council leave us facing the ICC," a Bashir spokesperson told the press. "It will be nothing less than ending all our agreements with the United Nations." Since the ICC has no international police force or military

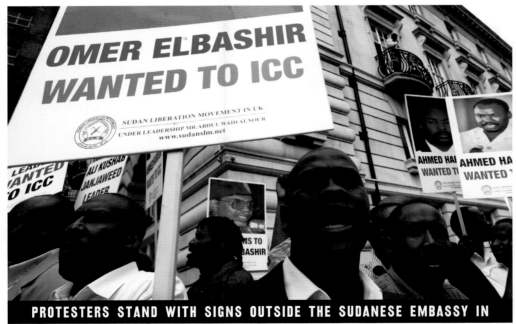

PROTESTERS STAND WITH SIGNS OUTSIDE THE SUDANESE EMBASSY IN London, England, in July 2008, after the International Criminal Court charged Bashir with murder, crimes against humanity, and genocide in Darfur.

> *"I support the opposition but I cannot accept what the ICC is doing. This is an indignity for all the people of Sudan. We are the people who should choose who our president is."*
>
> —Al-Siir Sabil, Khartoum taxi driver, July 2008

to carry out the arrest, Bashir does not have to fear being detained as long as he remains in Sudan or visits only countries opposed to the ICC's mandate. But will Bashir have enough support to stay in power if he cuts Sudan off completely from the UN and much of the international community?

The fate of Sudan as a country also hangs in the balance. If Bashir's dictatorship endures, southern Sudan will doubtless choose independence in the 2011 referendum. That is, if Bashir somehow does not find a way to prevent the referendum from taking place. If he does, Sudan may continue its history of crisis.

WHO'S WHO?

JOHN GARANG (1945–2005): Born in Upper Nile State into a Christian Dinka family, John Garang grew up during the first civil war (1955–1972) between northern and southern Sudan. He attended high school in Tanzania and later earned a B.A. in economics at Grinnell College in Iowa. While doing research in agricultural economics at the University of Dar es Salaam in Tanzania, he became active in the African Revolutionary Front, a student organization campaigning against colonialism. When he returned to Sudan, he joined the rebel army. After the war ended in 1972, he became a captain in the Sudanese army. He returned to the United States for military training at Fort Benning, Georgia, and later to earn a Ph.D. at Iowa State University. When civil war erupted again in 1983, Garang was called back to active duty. Sent to put down a revolt in Bor in southern Sudan, he instead joined the rebellion, founded the SPLM/A, and became its leader.

The Comprehensive Peace Agreement in 2005 gave Garang the presidency of the government of southern Sudan and the post of first vice president in the Government of National Unity, but he was killed in a helicopter crash three weeks after his inauguration. In spite of rumors of conspiracy and widespread protest, no forensic evidence has been found that the crash was anything but an accident.

SALVA KIIR MAYARDIT (1951–): Like John Garang, Salva Kiir Mayardit is a Dinka but comes from a different clan. During the 1960s, Kiir joined the Anya-Nya, the southern rebel group. When the conflict was settled in 1972, Kiir was accepted into the regular army. Eleven years later, when rebellion erupted again, Kiir, like Garang, left the army to join the rebels and was a founding member of the SPLM/A. Because Kiir had more experience in the field, Garang entrusted him with many military decisions. Kiir also played an important role in the peace negotiations in Nigeria and Kenya.

After years as Garang's dependable deputy, Kiir was suddenly thrown into the political spotlight when Garang died in 2005. Kiir succeeded Garang as president of southern Sudan and vice president of the Government of National Unity. Although Kiir had favored secession for the south, he promised to give priority to Garang's wish for a unified Sudan.

MINNI ARCUA MINNAWI (1972–): A Zaghawa from Darfur, Minnawi joined the Darfur rebellion as it was starting in late 2001 and soon rose to a leadership role in the Sudanese Liberation Movement/Army. Minnawi's knowledge of English, which he had learned while living with an uncle in Nigeria, often made him the principal SLA spokesperson to world media. Minnawi scored impressive military victories as the commander of Zaghawa troops who were veterans of wars in Chad, but he also became known for irresponsible attacks on peaceable Arab and non-Arab groups.

In 2005, when the SLM split into two factions, Minnawi became president of one faction. The founding leader of the movement, Abdel Wahid al-Nur led the other faction. Three rebel groups represented Darfur at the peace talks in Abuja, Nigeria: SLA-Minnawi, SLA-Wahid, and JEM, but only Minnawi signed the Darfur Peace Agreement in May 2006. He was appointed senior assistant to President Bashir. In 2008, however, Minnawi grew dissatisfied with the government's lack of progress in carrying out the terms of the agreement. He left Khartoum, vowing he would not return until he had evidence of "the good will of the dominant National Congress Party."

MUAMMAR AL-QADDAFI (1942–): Qaddafi has ruled Libya since 1969. In that year, in a bloodless coup, he overthrew King Idris I, who had led the country since its independence from Italian colonial rule in 1951. Qaddafi envisioned uniting the Arab world across northern Africa into a political system governed by thousands of people's committees. He sought to influence politics in Africa through military invasion and support for rebel groups, creating problems in Chad and Sudan, as well as

other countries. In recent years, Qaddafi has changed tactics from anti-Western revolutionary to international good guy. He has taken responsibility for earlier terrorist bombings and compensated victims, sent aid to impoverished countries, mediated conflicts in war-torn areas, and helped humanitarian assistance reach Darfur refugees in Chad. In February 2009, Qaddafi was elected chairman of the African Union. He seeks to promote the unification of Africa while in office.

SADIQ AL-MAHDI (1936–): The political and religious leader of the Umma Party and the Mahdist Brotherhood, Sadiq is a grandson of Abd al-Rahman al-Mahdi, a founder of independent Sudan, and a great-grandson of the Mahdi. Born in Omdurman and educated at both the University of Khartoum and Oxford University in Great Britain, Sadiq became head of the Umma Party on the death of his father in 1961. He served briefly as prime minister in 1966, during the second parliamentary administration. During Gaafar al-Nimeiri's dictatorship (1969–1985), Sadiq was frequently imprisoned or exiled. He was prime minister again from 1986 until Bashir's coup in 1989.

After the coup, Sadiq was often detained in prison and in ghost houses or confined to house arrest or to Khartoum. But he actively protested Bashir's dictatorship in sermons and in interviews published outside of Sudan, accusing Bashir of religious extremism, distortion of Islam, and abuse of human rights.

In 1996 Sadiq escaped from Khartoum and joined other exiled Sudanese politicians in Asmara, Eritrea. When Bashir allowed political parties once again to be openly active in Sudan, Sadiq returned to lead the Umma as an opposition party.

ALI OSMAN MUHAMMAD TAHA (1948–): The son of a zookeeper, Taha is a member of the Shayqiyya from the Nile Valley in northern Sudan. He studied law at the University of Khartoum, where he joined the Muslim Brotherhood and the Islamic Charter Front (later the National Islamic Front), becoming Turabi's second in command in 1987. As the NIF liaison to the army, Taha became the main plotter of Bashir's coup in

1989. Taha was imprisoned along with other Sudanese politicians, but he was soon free and chairing the shadowy Council of Forty. He has been credited with the policy of "Islamic total transformation," which included programs such as the PDF training, the peace villages, and the camps for street children. He became minister of social planning in 1993 and foreign minister in 1995. In 1998 Bashir chose him as vice president. He worked closely with John Garang in developing the Comprehensive Peace Agreement and became second vice president in 2005 when that agreement went into effect. In September 2008, Taha appeared at the United Nations General Assembly meeting in New York to request that the Security Council stop the indictment of Bashir by the International Criminal Court.

HASSAN AL-TURABI (1932–): Born in Kassala in eastern Sudan, Turabi is the son of a religious judge. He studied law at the University of Khartoum, where he became active in the Muslim Brotherhood. He earned a master's of law degree at the University of London, and a Ph.D. at the Sorbonne in Paris. On returning to Khartoum, he joined the faculty of law at the university and later became its chancellor. In 1965 Turabi resigned his post at the university to devote himself to politics. For the next five years, Turabi led the Islamic Charter Front.

During Nimeiri's dictatorship, Turabi spent six years in prison and three years in exile in Libya. When Nimeiri embraced Islamism, however, he welcomed Turabi back to Sudan and appointed him attorney general. Turabi actively enforced Nimeiri's unpopular Sharia laws.

In 1985 Turabi organized the National Islamic Front to gain a broader popular base for his party. He developed friendships with NIF sympathizers in the army and in 1989 used the army to gain power so that the NIF could not win in elections. He later called the coup "the failed 'NIF experiment.'" Since being ousted by Bashir in 1999, Turabi has become a leading opposition figure.

TIMELINE

1090 B.C.–A.D. 350   Nubian kings dominate the Nile Valley in northern Sudan.

1500s–1800s   Funj and Fur sultans rule most of northern Sudan.

1820–1822   Turkish and Egyptian forces conquer the Funj sultanate and establish Ottoman rule.

1881–1898   Islamic visionary the Mahdi leads a rebellion against Turkish rule. His successor unites northern Sudan into one Islamic state.

1899–1956   British forces lead the conquest of Mahdist Sudan and establish the Anglo-Egyptian Condominium. The British also gain control of southern Sudan.

1916   Darfur becomes part of the condominium when British forces defeat Darfuris.

1944   On January 1, Omar Hassan Ahmed al-Bashir is born in northeastern Sudan.

1955   The mutiny of a southern military unit marks the start of civil war.

1956   Sudan becomes an independent nation governed as a parliamentary republic.

1958–1964   Major General Ibrahim Abboud leads the first military regime.

1965–1969   A second parliamentary government led by the Umma Party rules Sudan.

1969   Colonel Gaafar al-Nimeiri and other officers seize the government in a bloodless coup.

1972   The civil war ends with a peace accord reached in Addis Ababa, Ethiopia.

1983 Nimeiri establishes Sharia law in Sudan. Southern dissidents form the SPLM/A and begin the second civil war.

1985 Nimeiri is overthrown, and a transitional government takes office.

1986–1989 A third parliamentary rule is led by Sadiq al-Mahdi.

1989 Bashir leads a successful military coup on June 30. He abolishes parliament, bans political parties, eliminates the free press, steps up assaults on rebels in the south, and begins making Sudan an Islamist state.

1993 Bashir dissolves the Revolutionary Command Council for National Salvation and names himself president of Sudan. The United States adds Sudan to its list of states that sponsor terrorism.

1994 Peace talks open in Nairobi, Kenya, with IGADD countries acting as mediators. Eritrea breaks off diplomatic relations with Sudan for aiding Eritrean rebels.

1995 Sudan is linked to an assassination attempt on Egyptian president Hosni Mubarak. Bashir travels to China, and China agrees to finance oil development.

1996 UN imposes sanctions on Sudan for involvement in the assassination attempt on Mubarak. Bashir wins presidential elections. Hassan al-Turabi becomes speaker of parliament. Osama bin Laden emigrates from Sudan to Afghanistan.

1997 An SPLM splinter group signs an agreement with the Bashir government. Its leaders become high officials in Khartoum. The U.S. increases sanctions on Sudan.

1998 A new constitution is adopted, and political associations are allowed. In southern Sudan, Nuer are forcibly relocated from oil regions.

1999 The first barrels of crude oil are exported from Sudan. Turabi introduces constitutional amendments to limit Bashir's power. Bashir declares a state of emergency and dissolves the legislature.

2000 Bashir is reelected president.

2001 Turabi is arrested on charges of threatening the security of Sudan.

2002 The government of Sudan and the SPLM sign a cease-fire agreement and road map to peace, the Machakos Protocol.

2003 An uprising begins in Darfur.

2004 U.S. secretary of state Colin L. Powell declares that the violence in Darfur is genocide.

2005 The government signs the Comprehensive Peace Agreement with the SPLM. Bashir is sworn in as the president of the Government of National Unity and SPLM chairman John Garang as first vice president. The Interim National Constitution is ratified. Garang dies in a helicopter crash and is succeeded by Salva Kiir Mayardit.

2006 The Minnawi faction of the rebel SLA signs the Darfur Peace Agreement with Bashir. The United Nations Security Council votes to send UN peacekeeping forces to Darfur.

2007 The International Criminal Court issues arrest warrants against Minister of the Interior Ahmad Harun and janjawiid leader Ali Kushayb for their alleged role in war crimes and crimes against humanity in Darfur.

2008 Luis Moreno-Ocampo, first prosecutor of the International Criminal Court, applies to the ICC in The Hague, Netherlands, for the indictment of Omar al-Bashir on charges of war crimes, crimes against humanity, and genocide.

2009 A panel of judges at the ICC issues a warrant for the arrest of President Bashir on charges of war crimes and crimes against humanity.

GLOSSARY

AU: African Union, an organization of fifty-three African countries. It replaced the OAU (Organization of African Unity) in 2002.

CPA: Comprehensive Peace Agreement, which settled the civil war between northern and southern Sudan in 2005

DUP: Democratic Unionist Party, the successor to the National Unionist Party

ghost house: a secret prison run by security forces

IGAD: Intergovernmental Authority on Development, a regional organization of seven countries located in the Sahel that mediated the peace talks during Sudan's civil war

Jaaliyyin: Arab Sudanese who claim descent from Ibrahim Jaal, a descendant of al-Abbas, uncle of the prophet Muhammad in Arabia. Most Jaaliyyin live in settled communities along the Nile.

janjawiid: an old western Sudanese nickname for bandits, often translated as "devils on horseback," which is applied to government-supported militias in Darfur

JEM: Justice and Equality Movement, rebel group in Darfur

murahaliin: militias of cattle herders (Baqqara) in south Sudan used as part of the PDF during the civil war

nazir: head of an ethnic group or large clan

NCP: National Congress Party, Bashir's political party, successor to the NIF

NDA: National Democratic Alliance, umbrella organization of Sudanese political parties, trade unions, and other groups opposed to the Bashir regime

NIF: National Islamic Front, Islamist party that backed Bashir's coup

NUP: National Unionist Party. In 1967 it became the Democratic Unionist Party (DUP).

PDF: Popular Defense Force, militias drafted by Bashir to support the regular army. The murahaliin and the janjawiid form part of the PDF.

PNC: Popular National Congress, splinter group of the National Congress Party started by Hassan al-Turabi in 2000

RCC: Revolutionary Command Council, the military junta in Sudan

Sahel: a transitional zone of semiarid grassland at the southern edge of the Sahara

Sharia: Islamic legal code based on the Quran and the Sunna (the sayings of the prophet Muhammad)

sheikh: Islamic scholar, or wise man

SLM/A: Sudanese Liberation Movement/Army, rebel group in Darfur

special rapporteur: an investigator appointed by the UN for a specific purpose or for a specific country. Since 1993 the UN Commission on Human Rights (since 2006, the Human Rights Council) has assigned four special rapporteurs to investigate and report on human rights abuses in Sudan.

SPLM/A: Sudanese People's Liberation Movement/Army, former rebels in the second civil war. After the war, the SPLM became the major political party in southern Sudan.

umda: head of a village or town

Umma: the political party of the Mahdist religious brotherhood

SOURCE NOTES

9 Neil Henry, "Sudanese Leader Consolidates Support within Military," *Washington Post*, July 2, 1989, A31.

9 Neil Henry, "Sudanese Military Forces Oust Mahdi Government in Coup," *Washington Post*, July 1, 1989, A12.

20 P. M. Holt and M. W. Daly, *A History of the Sudan: From the Coming of Islam to the Present Day*, 5th ed. (London: Longman, 2000), 39.

26 H. A. MacMichael, *The Anglo-Egyptian Sudan* (London: Faber and Faber, 1934), 274.

28 Holt and Daly, *A History of Sudan*, 126.

33 Robert O. Collins, *A History of Modern Sudan* (Cambridge: Cambridge University Press, 2008), 65.

39 Amir H. Idris, *Conflict and Politics of Identity in Sudan* (New York: Palgrave Macmillan, 2005), 52.

41 Collins, *A History of Modern Sudan*, 117.

43 J. Millard Burr and Robert O. Collins, *Requiem for the Sudan: War, Drought, and Disaster Relief on the Nile* (Boulder, CO: Westview Press, 1995), 207.

44 Holt and Daly, *A History of Sudan*, 179.

49 G. Norman Anderson, *Sudan in Crisis: The Failure of Democracy* (Gainesville: University Press of Florida, 1999), 255.

50 Burr and Collins, *Requiem*, 206.

52 Henry, "Sudanese Military Forces Oust Mahdi Government in Coup."

52 Peter Nyot Kok, *Governance and Conflict in the Sudan, 1985–1995* (Hamburg: Deutsches Orient-Institut, 1996), 243.

52 Burr and Collins, *Requiem*, 205.

52 BBC, "Profile: Sudan's President Bashir," *BBC News*, November 25, 2003, http://news.bbc.co.uk/2/hi/africa/3273569.stm (February 18, 2009).

52 Burr and Collins, *Requiem*, 206.

55 Neil Henry, "After Coup, Unsettled Sudan Faces Yet Another Fresh Start,"

Washington Post, July 15, 1989, A18.

56 Burr and Collins, *Requiem*, 250.

57 Henry, "After Coup, Unsettled Sudan Faces Yet Another Fresh Start."

57 Raymond Bonner, "Notes and Comment," *New Yorker*, May 28, 1990, 27.

58 Mohamed Elhachmi Hamdi, *The Making of an Islamic Political Leader: Conversations with Hasan al-Turabi*, translated by Arthur A. Shamis (Boulder, CO: Westview Press, 1998), 61.

58 Burr and Collins, *Requiem*, 307.

58 Raymond Bonner, "Letter from Sudan," *New Yorker*, July 13, 1992, 81.

59 Ibid., 82.

59 Hamdi, *The Making of an Islamic Political Leader: Conversations with Hasan al-Turabi*, 61.

60 Ann Mosely Lesch, *The Sudan: Contested National Identities* (Bloomington: University of Indiana Press, 1998), 115.

61 Kok, *Governance and Conflict in the Sudan, 1985–1995*, 103.

62 Reuters, "Islamic Rule Is Reaffirmed by Islamic Chief," *New York Times*, March 24, 1996.

63 James C. McKinley, Jr., "Sudanese Vote, Sourly, as Islamic Fervor Chafes," *New York Times*, March 16, 1996, A4.

66 Nicholas Coghlan, *Far in the Waste Sudan: On Assignment in Africa* (Montreal: McGill-Queen's University Press, 2005), 165.

67 *New York Times,* "Vote in Sudan Starts Slowly as Opposition Calls Boycott," December 14, 2000, A9.

68 Abdullahi A. Gallab, *The First Islamist Republic: Development and Disintegration of Islamism in the Sudan* (Burlington, VT: Ashgate Publishing Co., 2008), 154.

68 BBC, "Sudan Strongman Turabi Arrested," *BBC News*, February 21, 2001, http://news.bbc.co.uk/2/hi/africa/1182978.stm (February 18, 2009).

68 Donald Petterson, *Inside Sudan: Political Islam, Conflict, and Catastrophe*, rev. ed. (Boulder, CO: Westview Press, 2003), 163.

71 Julie Flint and Alex de Waal, *Darfur: A New History of a Long War*, rev. and updated (London: Zed Books, 2008), 47.

74 Joyce Apsel, ed., *Darfur: Genocide before Our Eyes* (New York: Institute for Study of Genocide, 2005), 78.

74 Embassy of the Republic of Sudan, "Darfur Conflict: Its History, Nature, and Development," *SudaNews*, June 2005, http://www.sudanembassy.org/pdf/sudanews05.pdf (February 19, 2009).

75 Marc Lacey, "Sudan and Southern Rebels Sign Deal Ending Civil War," *New York Times*, January 10, 2005, http://www.nytimes.com/2005/01/01/international/africa/01sudan.html (February 18, 2009).

76 James Bone, "Bashir 'Totally Rejects' UN Force," *Times* (London), September 20, 2006, http://www.timesonline.co.uk/tol/news/world/us_ and_americas/article645068.ece (February 18, 2009)

77 Jeffrey Gettleman, "As Charges Loom, Sudan Chief Mounts Charm Offensive," *New York Times*, July 24, 2008, A6.

77 BBC, "Warrant Issued for Sudan's Leader," *BBC News*, March 4, 2009, http://news.bbc.co.uk/2/hi/africa/7923102.stm (March 5, 2009).

80 Julie Flint, "Under Islamic Siege," *Africa Report*, September–October, 1993, 25.

80 Lesch, *The Sudan: Contested National Identities*, 138.

81 Petterson, *Inside Sudan*, 68–69.

81 Lisa Schlein, "UN: Human Rights Violations in Sudan's Darfur Province Worsening," *Voice of America News*, September 16, 2008, http://www.voanews.com/English/2008-09-16-voa58.cfm (February 18, 2009).

82 Jane Perlez, "Sudan Hardens Crackdown on Internal Opponents," *New York Times*, December 17, 1989, 23.

82 Bonner, "Letter from Sudan,"
    78.

83 Ibid., 80.

83 Lesch, *The Sudan*, 133.

84 Ann M. Lesch, "Khartoum
    Diary," *Middle East Report*
    (November–December 1989),
    37.

87 Coghlan, *Far in the Waste
    Sudan*, 36.

87 Gérard Prunier, *Darfur: The
    Ambiguous Genocide*, rev.
    and updated ed. (Ithaca, NY:
    Cornell University Press, 2007),
    177.

89 Jemera Rone, *Children in
    Sudan: Slaves, Street Children
    and Child Soldiers* (New York:
    Human Rights Watch, 1995), 45.

90 William Finnegan, "The
    Invisible War," *New Yorker*,
    January 25, 1999, 62.

91 Rone, *Children in Sudan*, 49.

95 Jeré Longman, "A Lost Boy of
    Sudan Could Find a Way to
    Beijing," *New York Times*, July 2,
    2008, C13.

98 Human Rights Watch/ Africa,
    "1995 Report on Sudan,"

hrw.org, 1995, http://www
.hrw.org/legacy/reports/1995/
WR95/AFRICA-10.htm
(February 18, 2009).

100 Curtis Francis Doebbler
    and Rifaat Osman Makkawi,
    comps., eds., and trans.,
    "Compilation of Selected
    Laws of Sudan," *Sudan Net*,
    1999, http://www.sudan.net/
    government/constitution/
    compile.html (February 18,
    2009).

100 Stephanie McCrummen,
    "Songs of Hope for Sudan,
    When the Censors Allow,"
    Washington Post, June 19, 2008,
    A12.

101 Doebbler and Makkawi,
    "Compilation of Selected Laws
    of Sudan."

102 Chris Hedges, "Sudan Presses
    Its Campaign to Impose
    Islamic Law on Non-Muslims,"
    New York Times, June 1, 1992,
    A6.

106 Lesch, *The Sudan*, 135.

107 Human Rights Watch, "World
    Report 1999, Africa, Sudan,"
    hrw.org, 1999, http://hrw.org/
    legacy/worldreport99/africa/

sudan.html (February 18, 2009).

112 Human Rights Watch/Africa, "Entrenching Impunity: Government Responsibility for International Crimes in Darfur," *hrw.org*, December 2005, http://www.hrw.org/en/reports/2005/12/08/entrenching-impunity (February 19, 2009).

116 Ghazi Suleiman and Curtis Francis Doebbler, "Human Rights in Sudan in the Wake of the New Constitution," *Human Rights Brief*, Fall 1998, http://www.wcl.american.edu/hrbrief/fall98/ghazi.html (February 18, 2009).

117 *New York Times,* "Vote in Sudan Starts Slowly as Opposition Calls Boycott," December 14, 2000, A9.

118 Kok, *Governance and Conflict in the Sudan, 1985–1995*, 99.

118 Burr and Collins, *Requiem*, 213.

120 Prunier, *Darfur: The Ambiguous Genocide*, 70.

125 United Nations, "United Nations Security Council Resolution 1054," *UN*, April 26, 1996, http://daccessdds.un.org/doc/UNDOC/GEN/N96/107/86/PDF/N9610786.pdf?OpenElement (October 24, 2008).

132 Julie Flint, "Under Islamic Siege," *Africa Report*, September–October 1993, 26.

132 Gamal Nkrumah, "Hassan Al-Turabi: Remaking History," *Al-Ahram Weekly Online*, May 11–17, 2006, http://weekly.ahram.org.eg/2006/794/profile.htm (February 18, 2009).

132 Lindsey Hilsum, "Channel 4—News—Interview: Omar al-Bashir," *Channel 4*, 2008, http://www.channel4.com/news/articles/politics/international_politics/interview+omar+al bashir/2562362?intcmp=rss_news_authors_lindsey_hilsum (February 18, 2009).

136 Sarah El Deeb, "Sudan to Lobby UN to Avert President's Prosecution," *wtop.com*, September 22, 2008, http://wtopnews.com/?nid=387&sid=1482636 (September 22, 2008).

137 Rob Crilly, "Darfur Indictment Prompts Coup Fears in Sudan," *Telegraph Media Group*, July 21, 2008, http://www.telegraph.co.uk/news/worldnews/africaandindianocean/sudan/2308829/Omar-al-Bashir-indictment-over-Darfur-prompts-coup-fears-in-Sudan.html (February 18, 2009).

139 *Sudan Tribune*, "Darfur Minnawi Returns to Sudanese Capital This Week: Report," October 14, 2008, http://www.sudantribune.com/spip.php?article28915 (February 18, 2009).

141 Nkrumah, "Hassan Al-Turabi: Remaking History."

SELECTED BIBLIOGRAPHY

Burr, J. Millard, and Robert O. Collins. *Darfur: The Long Road to Disaster*. Princeton, NJ: Markus Wiener, 2006.

_____. *Requiem for the Sudan: War, Drought, and Disaster Relief on the Nile*. Boulder, CO: Westview Press, 1995.

_____. *Revolutionary Sudan: Hasan al-Turabi and the Islamist State, 1989–2000*. Leiden, Netherlands: Brill, 2003.

Coghlan, Nicholas. *Far in the Waste Sudan: On Assignment in Africa*. Montreal: McGill-Queen's University Press, 2005.

Collins, Robert O. *A History of Modern Sudan*. Cambridge: Cambridge University Press, 2008.

Daly, M. W. *Darfur's Sorrow: A History of Destruction and Genocide*. Cambridge: Cambridge University Press, 2007.

Flint, Julie, and Alex de Waal. *Darfur: A New History of a Long War*. London: Zed Books, 2008.

Gallab, Abdullahi A. *The First Islamist Republic: Development and Disintegration of Islamism in the Sudan*. Burlington, VT: Ashgate Publishing Co., 2008.

Holt, P. M., and M. W. Daly. *A History of the Sudan: From the Coming of Islam to the Present Day*. 5th ed. London: Longman, 2000.

Idris, Amir H. *Conflict and Politics of Identity in Sudan*. New York: Palgrave Macmillan, 2005.

Johnson, Douglas. *The Root Causes of Sudan's Civil Wars*. Oxford, UK: James Currey, 2003.

Jok, Jok Madok. *Sudan: Race, Religion, and Violence*. Oxford, UK: Oneworld Publications, 2007.

Lesch, Ann Mosely. *The Sudan: Contested National Identities*. Bloomington: University of Indiana Press, 1998.

Lobban, Richard A., Jr., Robert S. Kramer, and Carolyn Fluehr-Lobban. *Historical Dictionary of the Sudan*. 3rd ed. Lanham, MD: Scarecrow Press, 2002.

Petterson, Donald. *Inside Sudan: Political Islam, Conflict, and Catastrophe*. Rev. ed. Boulder, CO: Westview Press, 2003.

Prunier, Gérard. *Darfur, The Ambiguous Genocide*. Rev. and updated ed. Ithaca, NY: Cornell University Press, 2007.

Sidahmed, Abdel Salam. *Politics and Islam in Contemporary Sudan*. New York: St. Martin's Press, 1996.

Warburg, Gabriel. *Islam, Sectarianism and Politics in Sudan Since the Mahdiyya*. London: Hurst & Company, 2003.

FURTHER READING & WEBSITES

BOOKS
NONFICTION

Bashir, Halima. *Tears of the Desert: A Memoir of Survival in Darfur.* With Damien Lewis. New York: Ballantine Books, 2008. A Zaghawa doctor writes of her childhood in Darfur, her medical training in Khartoum, and her firsthand experiences of the horrors of the war in Darfur.

Bok, Francis. *Escape from Slavery: The True Story of My Ten Years in Captivity and My Journey to Freedom in America.* With Edward Tivnan. New York: St. Martin's Press, 2003. Bok relates his capture at the age of seven, his years of slavery, and his long odyssey to freedom.

Deng, Benson, Alephonson Deng, and Benjamin Ajak. *They Poured Fire on Us from the Sky.* With Judy A. Bernstein. New York: Public Affairs, 2005. The true story of three Lost Boys of Sudan who escaped the violence of the civil war in southern Sudan, walked 1,000 miles (1,600 km) through unimaginable dangers to a refugee camp in Kenya, and later immigrated to the United States.

DiPiazza, Francesca. *Sudan in Pictures.* Minneapolis: Twenty-First Century Books, 2006. This title in the Visual Geography series introduces Sudan's geography, people, history, government, economy, and cultural life.

Hari, Daoud. *The Translator: A Tribesman's Memoir of Darfur.* As told to Dennis Michael Burke and Meghan M. McKenna. New York: Random House, 2008. A Zaghawa tribesman writes of his work as a translator for international aid groups and reporters covering the war in Darfur.

Marlowe, Jen, Aisha Bain, and Adam Shapiro. *Darfur Diaries: Stories of Survival. New York: Nation Books, 2006.* Three young filmmakers recount their experiences making a documentary about the war in Darfur.

Walzer, Craig, ed. *Out of Exile: The Abducted and Displaced People of Sudan.* New York: McSweeney's, 2008. Refugees, displaced people,

and slaves captured during Sudan's civil war recount in their own
words their escapes from persecution and from abduction, describing
the wars in Darfur and southern Sudan and their lives in IDP camps
and in exile.

FICTION

Applegate, Katherine. *Home of the Brave*. New York: Feiwel and Friends,
2007. This novel in verse tells the story of a boy and his teenage
cousin, refugees from the civil war in Sudan, adapting to life in
Minnesota.

Eggers, Dave. *What Is the What*. New York: Vintage, 2007. A novel based
on the experiences of Valentino Achak Deng (one of the Lost Boys of
Sudan) who came to the United States in 2001.

Levitin, Sonia. *Dream Freedom*. New York: Silverwhistle, 2000. This novel
alternates between the story of a fifth-grade class in the United States
raising money to free slaves in Sudan and vignettes of Sudanese life
that show the complexity of the slavery issue.

WEBSITES

Darfur Relief and Documentation Centre
   http://www.darfurcentre.ch
   The DRDC is a nongovernmental organization in Geneva, Switzerland,
   established in 2004 to help bring peace to Darfur. The site has reports
   and documents relating to the crisis.

Gurtong Trust
   http://www.gurtong.org
   An outgrowth of the Gurtong Peace Trust Project, an independent
   nongovernmental organization, this site is devoted to promoting unity
   and peace among the peoples of southern Sudan. It offers information
   about arts and culture, ethnic groups, government, health, education,
   and travel in southern Sudan.

Human Rights Watch

http:// www.hrw.org

This independent nongovernmental organization, founded in 1978 and based in the United States, monitors human rights issues in more than seventy countries around the world, conducting fact-finding investigations and publishing the results in books and reports that are available online. The site carries annual reports and frequent updates on Sudan.

Sudan Net

http://sudan.net

This site, in English and Arabic, offers a variety of information about Sudan, recent news, discussion boards, Sudanese music, and 474 links to other Sudan-related sites.

Sudan Research, Analysis, and Advocacy

http://www.sudanreeves.org

American Eric Reeves, a Sudan activist, posts commentary on news concerning Sudan. The site includes photos, his magazine and newspaper articles, and congressional testimony.

Sudan Tribune

http://www.sudantribune.com

A nonprofit website based in France, *Sudan Tribune* publishes news in English about Sudan from many sources, commentary on the news, and documents relating to Sudanese issues. The site also invites comments from visitors.

Sudan Update

http:// www.sudanupdate.org

A nonpartisan, independent media review since June 1989, Sudan Update summarizes news and commentary about current events in Sudan from publications and broadcasts in Arabic, French, Italian, German, and English. It also publishes online reports of international conferences on Sudanese issues, such as slavery, oil, women's rights, and minorities.

Sudan Watch

http://sudanwatch.blogspot.com

British blogger Ingrid Jones has been posting news items about Sudan and her commentary on them since 2003.

vgsbooks.com

http://www.vgsbooks.com

This home page for Lerner Publishing Group's Visual Geography Series® provides links to online information, including geographical, historical, demographic, cultural, and economic websites, as well as late-breaking news, for 96 countries.

DOCUMENTARY FILMS

Bain, Aisha, and Jen Marlowe. *Darfur Diaries: Message from Home*. DVD. Canoga Park, CA: Cinema Libre, 2006. Victims of Darfur's violence speak about their experiences.

Quinn, Christopher, and Tommy Walker. *God Grew Tired of Us*. DVD. Culver City, CA: Sony Pictures, 2007. The directors follow three young Sudanese men, John Bul Dau, Panther Bior, and Daniel Abul Pach, as they grapple with the difficulties of relocating to the United States after years spent in refugee camps.

Shenk, John, and Megan Mylan. *POV: Lost Boys of Sudan*. DVD. New York: New Video Group, 2004. Two teenage Sudanese refugees, Peter Kon Dut and Santino Majok Chuor, resettle in Houston, Texas.

Sundberg, Annie, and Rikki Stern. *The Devil Came on Horseback*. DVD. New York: International Film Circuit / Break Thru Films, 2007. Former Marine captain Brian Steidle narrates his experiences as a member of the AU troops monitoring the cease-fire in the Nuba Mountains and Darfur in 2004, with photographs taken on his mission and later footage filmed by the directors.

Thomas, Dwain. *Facing Sudan*. DVD. Cary, IL: Bell, Book & Camera Productions, 2008. The second Sudanese civil war (1983–2005) is explained with video footage and interviews of survivors.

INDEX

AUTHOR BIOGRAPHY

Diana Childress has written nine books and dozens of magazine articles for children and young adults, mainly on historical topics. Recent published titles include *Pinochet's Chile* (Dictatorships series), *Johannes Gutenberg and the Printing Press* (Pivotal Moments in History), and *Barefoot Conquistador*, a biography of the sixteenth-century Spanish explorer Álvar Núñez Cabeza de Vaca. She lives in New York City.

PHOTO ACKNOWLEDGMENTS